W9-DGI-213

Solutions to Social Problems
from the Bottom Up
Successful Social Movements

D. STANLEY EITZEN
Emeritus, Colorado State University

KENNETH STEWART
Angelo State University

PEARSON

Boston • New York • San Francisco
Mexico City • Montreal • Toronto • London • Madrid • Munich • Paris
Hong Kong • Singapore • Tokyo • Cape Town • Sydney

Senior Series Editor: Jeff Lasser
Series Editorial Assistant: Erikka Adams
Senior Marketing Manager: Kelly May
Editorial Production Service: Omegatype Typography, Inc.
Composition Buyer: Linda Cox
Manufacturing Buyer: JoAnne Sweeney
Electronic Composition: Omegatype Typography, Inc.
Cover Administrator: Elena Sidorova

For related titles and support materials, visit our online catalog at www.ablongman.com.

Copyright © 2007 Pearson Education, Inc.

All rights reserved. No part of the material protected by this copyright notice may be reproduced or utilized in any form or by any means, electronic or mechanical, including photocopying, recording, or by any information storage and retrieval system, without written permission of from the copyright owner.

To obtain permission(s) to use material from this work, please submit a written request to Allyn and Bacon, Permissions Department, 75 Arlington Street, Boston, MA 02116 or fax your request to 617-848-7320.

Between the time website information is gathered and then published, it is not unusual for some sites to have closed. Also, the transcription of URLs can result in typographical errors. The publisher would appreciate notification where these errors occur so that they may be corrected in subsequent editions.

Library of Congress Cataloging-in-Publication Data

Solutions to social problems from the bottom up: successful social movements / [edited by] D. Stanley Eitzen, Kenneth Stewart.—1st ed.
　　p. cm.
　Includes bibliographical references.
　ISBN 0-205-46884-5 (pbk.)
　1. Social movements.   2. Social movements—United States.   3. Social Problems.
　4. Social problems—United States.   I. Eitzen, D. Stanley.   II. Stewart, Kenneth L.
　HM881.S65 2008
　303.48′409—dc22   2006052455

Printed in the United States of America

Contents

PREFACE

This book is part of a series on solutions to social problems in the United States. The first book, *Solutions to Social Problems: Lessons from Other Societies*, provides examples of how other advanced industrial societies have dealt with social problems with relative success, implying that their strategies may be applicable to the United States. The second book, *Solutions to Social Problems from the Top Down: The Role of Government*, examines U.S. history to describe government programs that have ameliorated social problems. The lesson is that the government, although not a perfect instrument, has on occasion made progressive changes for the common good. This book, *Solutions to Social Problems from the Bottom Up: Successful Social Movements*, focuses on how solutions to social problems have emerged from the people as they have joined with others.

Social movements are intriguing because they are efforts by the powerless to challenge and confront the powerful and demand meaningful change. This is a seemingly impossible task. But armed with an ideology, sufficient numbers, a strong organization, and a strategy, weak groups such as racial minorities, welfare mothers, migrant workers, sweatshop workers, and janitors can win against unfair laws and unfair practices. Thus, social movements are an essential part of a truly democratic society.

As the introductory essay indicates, there are three kinds of social movements—those that resist or reverse social change, those that seek to alter social institutions, and those that seek the transformation of society. This book focuses on the second type—reform movements. Although there are movements aimed at all kinds of reform, we limit our examination to progressive social movements that have sought to redress social problems such as barriers to class, race, and gender equality, democratic practices, economic advancement, and social justice. Chapter 1 incorporates articles on the importance of social movements. Chapter 2 looks at social movements that have promoted race, class, and gender equality. Chapter 3 examines those that enhanced democracy and equal access to power. Chapter 4 focuses on movements that pressed for corporate social responsibility. Chapter 5 describes a new generation of social movements seeking to advance social justice in today's globalized world. In each of these chapters involving solutions to social problems, we want to show the positive "building" aspects of movements, not just the negative "being against" aspects. The final chapter is a plea for citizen involvement in social movements for the benefit of the common good.

Each chapter introduces a topic and contains selected readings that generally describe particular movements, their leadership, or other manifestations of a successful movement.

This book is intended to supplement traditional social problems textbooks, which typically are long on descriptive content of social problems but short on solutions. It will be a useful supplement in other sociology courses such as political sociology, collective behavior, social policy, and social change. The book also fits with courses in other disciplines, most notably history and political science.

ACKNOWLEDGMENTS

We are indebted to Jeff Lasser, sociology editor at Allyn and Bacon, whose ideas initiated this project. Others who have influenced the project are Maxine Baca Zinn, Craig Leedham, George H. Sage, Kathryn Talley, Doug Timmer, and John Wheeler. Our thanks to them for their insights and inspiration.

As editors of this volume, we desire to promote a more democratic society for the United States, one that truly reflects the "will of the people." We are inspired by the people who took part in the many bottom-up social movements that are the subject of this text. This book is dedicated to them.

D.S.E.
K.L.S.

CHAPTER 1

Social Movements
and Democracy

If you are trying to transform a brutalized society into one where people can live with dignity and hope, you begin with the empowering of the most powerless. You build from the bottom up.

—Adrienne Rich

History is the long and tragic story of the fact that privileged groups seldom give up their privileges voluntarily.... We know through painful experience that freedom is never voluntarily given by the oppressor; it must be demanded by the oppressed....

—Martin Luther King, Jr.

One of the dangers of talking about the structural sources of social change or its cultural, environment, and institutional consequences is that we then tend to see change as a purely macrolevel, structural phenomenon, something that happens to us rather than something we create. But social change is not some huge, invisible hand that descends from the heavens to arbitrarily disrupt our routine way of life. It is, in the end, a phenomenon driven by human action.

—David M. Newman

Perhaps people can begin, here and there (not waiting for the government, but leading it)....

—Howard Zinn

The South in the 1950s was rigidly segregated by custom and law. Restaurants, hotels, and stores were only allowed to serve whites. There were black-only water fountains, black-only elevators, black-only schools, and hundreds of other ways that blacks were treated as inferior to whites. Jim Crow tests were designed to keep blacks from voting. Individuals and organizations such as the Ku Klux

Klan used violence, including lynchings, to intimidate blacks to stay "in their place." On December 1, 1955, an African American woman named Rosa Parks refused to give up her seat to a white man on a Montgomery, Alabama, city bus. The rules were that the first four rows on the bus were for whites only. Blacks were to sit in the back of the bus. Between these white and black worlds was a middle section. Blacks could sit there, but if a white person needed the seat, the black passenger was to vacate that seat and the whole row, to spare the white person the embarrassment of sitting next to an "inferior" person. The bus driver asked Rosa Parks to give up her seat in this middle section but she refused. She was arrested and convicted for violating a city ordinance and behaving in a disorderly manner.

This simple act of civil disobedience by one person set off a chain of events that changed the South. Following Ms. Parks's arrest, more than 5,000 people packed a church and passed a resolution backing a bus boycott. They chose a 26-year-old pastor as their leader—Martin Luther King, Jr. Six weeks later the home of Martin Luther King, Jr., was bombed. The boycott lasted 381 days, with blacks walking, car pooling, and bicycling instead of using public transportation. Rallies were held, newsletters distributed, and court cases initiated. Eleven months after Ms. Parks's arrest, the Supreme Court ruled that segregation on public transportation was illegal. The boycott ended a month later, after federal injunctions enforced the court's ruling. The Montgomery bus boycott, which involved over 40,000 blacks, was the beginning of the modern civil rights movement. With Martin Luther King, Jr. as the charismatic spokesman, and many thousands of courageous protestors keeping the pressure on through passive resistance, other forms of discrimination also broke down. The success of the movement culminated a decade after Rosa Parks's defiant act with the passage of the historic Civil Rights Act of 1964 and the Voting Rights Act of 1965 (Kotz, 2005). What began as one woman insisting on being treated fairly, despite laws that mandated that she be treated unfairly, altered history and the "ugly system of U.S. apartheid fell" (*USA Today*, 2005:11A). Jesse Jackson put it this way: "She sat down in order that we all might stand up, and the walls of segregation came down" (quoted in Willing, 2005:2A). In 1996, Rosa Parks received the Presidential Medal of Freedom, followed three years later with the Congressional Gold Medal of Honor, the two highest honors that can be bestowed on a civilian.

The civil rights movement is a classic example of a powerless group of people who were disenfranchised and considered second class by the powerful majority, yet they were able to win against seemingly overwhelming odds. Throughout the history of the United States, oppressed groups have organized to challenge their oppressors and change history. It all began when the colonists defeated the mighty British Empire, leading to a sovereign United States. In the late 1800s, against huge and often violent resistance by employers, workers organized unions and achieved higher wages, an eight-hour work day, and safer working conditions. After many years of petitions, demonstrations, and other grassroots efforts, women finally achieved the right to vote in 1919. In each of these examples and countless others, the powerless took on the powerful and succeeded against great odds. Not even a Rosa Parks or a Martin Luther King, Jr. could bring about such social change alone. In each instance it took the collective efforts of many to accomplish the goal.

This book describes collective efforts by powerless people in U.S. history that have promoted equality, democracy, corporate social responsibility, and social justice. These collective efforts to bring about social change are called *social movements*.

WHAT IS A SOCIAL MOVEMENT?

The formal definition of a social movement is the collective attempt to promote, resist, or reverse change. Individuals seeking to change social life in some meaningful way are limited in what they can accomplish by themselves. For success, those who share similar goals must join together.

> *As individuals, we are limited in our ability to make the societal changes we would like. There are massive social forces that make change difficult; these forces include the government, large and powerful organizations, and the prevailing values, norms, and attitudes. As individuals going to a voting booth, we have minimal power. As individuals protesting to officials, we have minimal power. As individuals standing against the tide of public opinion, we have little hope of exerting influence. As individuals confronting a corporate structure, we are doomed to frustration and failure. But if we combine with others who share our convictions, organize ourselves, and map out a course of action, we may be able to bring about numerous and significant changes in the social order. Through participation in a social movement, we can break through the social constraints that overwhelm us as individuals. (Kammeryer, Ritzer, and Yetman, 1997:632–633)*

Social movements arise when people are sufficiently discontented and angry at the status quo. As William Sloan Coffin wrote, "you cannot have a revolt without revolting conditions" (Coffin, 2004:62). Clearly, Rosa Parks and her black sisters and brothers who participated in the Montgomery bus boycott were willing to face adversity, even violence, because of their hatred of the unjust system that demeaned them in so many ways.

A social movement is a goal-directed effort by a substantial number of people. It is an enduring organization with leaders, a division of labor, an ideology, a blueprint for collective action, and a set of roles and norms for the members (Blumer, 1951; Smelser, 1962). The activities of the members may include donating money, signing petitions, demonstrating and protesting without violence, and rioting. Although strategies and organizational skills are important, ideology is the key to a movement's success. The ideology provides the goal and the rationale for action, binds diverse members together in a common cause, and submerges individuals in the movement. It also identifies people as either allies or enemies. An ideology may be elaborate, such as Christianity, Marxism, or capitalism. Such an ideology provides a consistent framework from which to act on and believe in a number of sweeping issues. Or the ideology may be narrowly aimed at one side or the other on issues such as animal rights, abortion, protection of the environment, capital punishment, gun control, gay rights, universal health insurance, or a living wage. For each of these issues, groups on either side have an ideology that explains their position, provides the goal, unites members, and offers a compelling argument for recruiting new members.

TYPES OF SOCIAL MOVEMENTS

Three types of social movements are political in nature: resistance movements, which are organized to resist changes; reform movements, which seek to alter a specific part of society; and revolutionary movements, which seek radical changes.

Because periods of rapid change foster resistance movements, there are numerous contemporary examples of this phenomenon. Antiabortion groups have formed to reverse legislation and judicial acts that make abortion legal or easy to obtain. Evangelicals in a number of communities have organized to pressure school boards to reverse school policies that they believe oppose Christian principles. They oppose the teaching of evolution and seek to have the schools teach creationism or intelligent design. They want prayer in the schools. They oppose teaching sex education unless the program only teaches abstinence. These groups are also convinced that the foundations of family life are eroding with women working outside the home, "no fault" divorce laws, the increasing acceptance of gays and lesbians, and, it follows, marriage between homosexuals.

Reform movements aim at altering a specific part of society. These movements commonly focus on a single issue, such as women's rights, gay rights, or global warming. Typically there is an aggrieved group such as women, African Americans, Native Americans, gays, people with disabilities, farmers, or workers. The civil rights movement of the 1950s and 1960s is a prime example of a reform movement. This book focuses on reform movements.

Unlike reform and resistance movements, the goal of the third type of social movement—the revolutionary movement—is radical change. Such movements go beyond reform by seeking to replace the existing social institutions with new ones that conform to a radically different vision of society. The American Revolution, the peasant uprising that overthrew the aristocracy in the French Revolution, the Bolshevik overthrow of the monarchy in Russia, the Communist Revolution in

China, and Castro's overthrow of Batista's government that replaced capitalism with a Marxist regime in Cuba are examples of revolutionary movements.

THE LIFE COURSE OF SOCIAL MOVEMENTS

Social movements move through stages. For a movement to begin, it must attract members. Typically there is some societal condition—institutional racism, sexism, economic depression, war, a wave of immigration, the passage of a controversial law or court decision, technological change—that threatens or harms some segment of society. Whatever the grievances, large numbers of people question the legitimacy of the status quo and demand change. This causes social unrest, but it is relatively unfocused.

The second stage of a movement is when grievances become focused. This occurs when there is some incident such as police brutality being caught on videotape, fire hoses being directed at peaceful demonstrators, churches being bombed, or Rosa Parks being fined and jailed for not giving up her seat on the bus in Montgomery. Such an event provides the spark that ignites a movement by turning moral outrage into political action. Under these conditions, social movements require leaders to emerge who use ideology and charisma to define the central problems and to challenge and inspire followers to join in a common quest to change society for the better. Sometimes there are individuals whose acts of personal courage, such as provoking the powerful, or being jailed, injured, or killed, serve to coalesce the previously unfocused. This is especially important in an age of instant communication, in which public attention is centered on the charismatic leader's message and personal valor, the heroism of martyrs, the repressive acts by authorities, the brutality of those opposing the movement, and the continuing inequities or injustices in society on which the movement is centered. This is a critical stage when those in similar situations realize that others share their feelings of discontent and anger, and that together they can make a difference. They begin to acquire a collective identity, a sense of common purpose, and a keen awareness of the "enemy." It is a time of excitement over the possibilities for collectively bringing about needed social change. This excitement leads many to exert extraordinary energies and to take risks that they might not have previously thought possible.

The third phase involves moving toward organization. Resources (money, equipment, and members) are mobilized. A formal organizational structure emerges with rules, policies, and procedures. Power is centralized and levels of organization are delineated. Communication networks are established (newsletters, weblogs, meetings). Strategies are formed to confront the authorities, attract new members, and keep older members energized. Alliances may be formed with other groups with similar goals. In short, this is a bureaucratization stage in which a once unfocused number of people now have become an organization. Whereas leadership was once charismatic, it is now composed of administrators and managers. The charismatic leadership that originally brought the movement together is "routinized."

Success depends, most importantly, on having organization and communication networks to mobilize supporters and to use the media to convince the public to be sympathetic to the movement. David M. Newman says that long-term success depends on the support of large organizations with connections to the political system.

> Those movements that historically have lasted longest—the women's movement, the civil rights movement, and the environmental movement—are those that are supported by large organizations. The National Organization of Women, the NAACP, the Sierra Club, and the like have full-time lobbyists or political action committees that connect them to the national political system. Few movements can succeed without such connections because achieving social change often requires changing laws or convincing courts to interpret laws in particular ways. (Newman, 2000:234)

The final stage occurs only if the movement is successful. The movement becomes integrated into society. The goals of the movement are accomplished, at least in some compromised form. This is the stage of institutionalization. Although this is the goal of the social movement, this stage has its dangers. A common danger is goal displacement. This occurs when the goal of maintaining the formal structure of the movement's organization supersedes the original goals of the social movement itself. Another threat involves power struggles within the movement as factions divide over tactics. In the civil rights movement, for example, Martin Luther King, Jr.'s tactic of nonviolence was challenged by the more aggressive Student Non-Violent Coordinating Committee, whose leader, Stokeley Carmichael, argued for more militant tactics. Even more extreme in their call for violence were Malcolm X of the Black Muslims and Huey P. Newton of the Black Panthers. The result of the differences among these splinter groups is the fragmentation of the original movement and the loss of effectiveness.

Success also can lead to the leadership elite using their power to retain power and the extraordinary status and reward that accompany that power. When this happens, the original goals of the movement have been corrupted. Finally, with success, social movements can become fixtures in society. As Newman observes, "Ironically, a social phenomenon whose goal is the large-scale alteration of some aspect of society can, in time, become part of the establishment it seeks to change" (Newman, 2000:535).

REPRISE: SOCIAL CHANGE FROM THE BOTTOM UP

Let's summarize what we know about the nature of social reform movements—the focus of this book. First, people have the potential to change society. Social relations are based on the cooperation, consent, or acquiescence of the people.

The powerful stay in power when the powerless go to work, pay their taxes, buy products, and obey the laws. "Social movements can be understood as the collective withdrawal of consent to established institutions" (Brecher, Costello, and Smith, 2000:21). This withdrawal of consent can take many forms—strikes, boycotts, civil disobedience, disobeying authority, challenging the law, and so forth. Activists often are chastised and vilified by conservatives who label them rogues, traitors, communists, sell-outs, America haters, or otherwise anti-American. Likewise, liberals sometimes elevate activists to something approaching saint-like purity, portraying them as freedom-fighters bearing crosses alone, bringing justice and liberty to ordinary people from the bottom up. Such is the politics of image-making that surrounds the legacies of national and international activists like Martin Luther King, Jr., Cesar Chavez, Eugene Debs, Che Guevara, Mahatma Gandhi, or Nelson Mandela.

In reality, social movement activists are usually neither pure nor villainous. Most often they are simply human beings who have personality flaws and quirks, who make deals and compromises for their causes, and who sometimes behave contrary to their own ideals. The personal intrigues of activists make great fodder for media stories, and the merits of progressive social movements are often weighed mostly in terms of the perceived virtues and vices of individuals who become activist leaders. From a sociological viewpoint, however, this mode of assessing movements is shallow because it focuses too narrowly on individuals rather than on the structural sources of movements and their consequences for social change. A more structural focus on social movements reveals that the powerless can, in certain circumstances, exercise their power with astonishing results.

The most important structural feature of progressive social movements is that they are political. Movements challenge and change existing power arrangements, always triggering tension between the powerful, who value and benefit from public order and stability, and the relatively powerless, who demand transformation of the status quo.

Because progressive social movements challenge power, they are ultimately essential to a democracy. They are expressions of the public will or some significant segment of the public (Tilly, 2004:36). In a democracy the people are theoretically the rulers. Social movements assert popular sovereignty. Ironically, though, the representatives of the people—government authorities—typically use their power to stifle dissent. Indeed, "America is a country—and a culture—founded on dissent. The nation was born in the most obvious form of protest, an armed rebellion against the legal authority of the day" (Hayden, 2004:46).

The authors that are featured in this chapter explore the crucial contributions that progressive social movements make to democracy. The actions of individual activists are only tangents to the readings. Instead, the authors identify the indispensable contributions of movements to solving social problems in ways that include the people, from the bottom up.

The first reading is David S. Meyer's "How Social Movements Matter." This article focuses on the current sociological understanding of social problems—the thesis that social problems focus around public policies designed and instituted by political and economic leaders. Meyer details not only the immediate influences of movements on public policies (which are often limited and disappointing to movement followers), but also the more implicit and long-range ways that progressive movements challenge problems inherent in the designs of leadership.

Our second author, historian Howard Zinn, takes up another important theme—the crucial role of dissent in progressive social movements. In the 1950s, psychologist Stanley Milgram conducted a now famous set of "shock experiments" showing how experimental subjects (American college students) could, against their better sensibilities, commit atrocities under effective leadership influences. Superficially, many people deny that leaders can have such influence on their behavior, but Milgram showed otherwise. Zinn addresses this aspect of authority and power in "The Problem Is Civil Obedience." Zinn shows how progressive social movements counteract the invisible pressures of power and authority to conform. He also shows how democratic solutions to social problems cannot occur without a structure that makes room for people to actively disobey authority.

REFERENCES

Blumer, Herbert. 1951. "Collective Behavior." In *Principles of Sociology*, 2nd ed., Alfred McClung Lee (ed.). New York: Barnes and Noble, pp. 167–222.

Brecher, Jeremy, Tim Costello, and Brendan Smith. 2000. *Globalization from Below: The Power of Solidarity*. Cambridge, MA: South End Press.

Coffin, William Sloan. 2004. *Credo*. Louisville, KY: Westminster John Knox Press.

Hayden, Thomas. 2004. "Dissent: Agreeing to Disagree." *U.S. News & World Report* (June 28/July 5):46–48.

Kammeyer, Kenneth C. W., George Ritzer, and Norman R. Yetman. 1997. *Sociology*, 7th ed. Boston: Allyn and Bacon.

Kotz, Nick. 2005. *Judgment Days: Lyndon Baines Johnson, Martin Luther King Jr., and the Laws That Changed America*. Boston: Houghton Mifflin.

Newman, David M. 2000. *Sociology: Exploring the Architecture of Everyday Life*, 3rd ed. Thousand Oaks, CA: Pine Forge Press.

Smelser, Neil. 1962. *Theory of Collective Behavior*. New York: Free Press.

Tilly, Charles. 2004. *Social Movements, 1768–2004*. Boulder, CO: Paradigm Publishers.

USA Today. 2005. "One Ordinary Woman, One Extraordinary Legacy." Editorial (October 25), 11A.

Willing, Richard. 2005. "Pioneer of Civil Rights Was 'A Real Person, Too,' " *USA Today* (October 26):2A.

How Social Movements Matter

DAVID S. MEYER

In January 2003, tens if not hundreds of thousands of people assembled in Washington, D.C. to try to stop the impending invasion of Iraq. It did not look good for the demonstrators. Months earlier, Congress authorized President Bush to use force to disarm Iraq, and Bush repeatedly said that he would not let the lack of international support influence his decision about when—or whether—to use military force. Opposition to military action grew in the intervening months; the Washington demonstration coincided with sister events in San Francisco, Portland, Tampa, Tokyo, Paris, Cairo, and Moscow. Protests, albeit smaller and less frequent, continued after the war began. Did any of them change anything? Could they have? How? And how would we know if they did?

Such questions are not specific to this latest peace mobilization, but are endemic to protest movements more generally. Social movements are organized challenges to authorities that use a broad range of tactics, both inside and outside of conventional politics, in an effort to promote social and political change. Opponents of the Iraq War wrote letters to elected officials and editors of newspapers, called talk radio shows and contributed money to antiwar groups. Many also invited arrest by civil disobedience: some protesters, for example, blocked entrances to government offices and military bases. A group of 50 "Unreasonable Women of West Marin" lay naked on a northern California beach, spelling out "Peace" with their bodies for a photographer flying overhead. Besides using diverse methods of protest, opponents of the war also held diverse political views. Some opposed all war, some opposed all U.S. military intervention, while others were skeptical only about this particular military intervention. This is a familiar social movement story: broad coalitions stage social movements, and differences within a movement coalition are often nearly as broad as those between the movement and the authorities it challenges.

Political activists and their targets act as if social movements matter, and sociologists have been trying, for the better part of at least four decades, to figure

Source: David S. Meyer, "How Social Movements Matter." *Contexts,* 2(4):30–35. © 2003, American Sociological Association. Used by permission of the University of California press and David S. Meyer.

out why, when and how. It is too easy—and not very helpful—to paint activists as heroes or; alternatively, as cranks. It is similarly too easy to credit them for social change or, alternatively, to dismiss their efforts by saying that changes, such as advances in civil rights or environmental protections, would have happened anyway. What we have learned is that social movements are less a departure from conventional institutional politics than an extension of them—a "politics by other means." In the end, we find that movements crest and wane, often failing to attain their immediate goals, but they can lastingly change political debates, governmental institutions and the wider culture.

It is often difficult to tell whether activism makes a difference because the forces that propel people to mobilize are often the same forces responsible for social change. For example, it is difficult to decide whether the feminist movement opened new opportunities to women or whether economic changes fostered both the jobs and feminism. Also, authorities challenged by movements deny that activism influenced their decisions. What politicians want to admit that their judgments can be affected by "mobs"? Why risk encouraging protesters in the future? Finally, movements virtually never achieve all that their partisans demand, and so activists are quick to question their own influence. As a result, proving that movements influence politics and policy involves difficult detective work.

But research shows that social movements can affect government policy, as well as how it is made, and movement influence extends further. Activism often profoundly changes the activists, and through them, the organizations in which they participate, as well as the broader culture. The ways that movements make a difference are complex, veiled, and take far longer to manifest themselves than the news cycle that covers a single demonstration, or even a whole protest campaign.

WHEN MOVEMENTS EMERGE

Activists protest when they think it might help them achieve their goals—goals they might not accomplish otherwise. Organizers successfully mobilize movements when they convince people that the issue at hand is urgent, that positive outcomes are possible and that their efforts could make a difference. In the case of the war on Iraq, for example, President Bush set the agenda for a broad range of activists by explicitly committing the country to military intervention. More conventional politics—elections, campaign contributions and letter-writing—had already played out and it became clear that none of these activities were sufficient, in and of themselves, to stop the war. In addition, the President's failure to build broad international or domestic support led activists to believe that direct pressure might prevent war. The rapid worldwide growth of the movement itself encouraged activism, assuring participants that they were part of something larger than themselves, something that might matter. In effect, President Bush's actions encouraged anti-war activism to spread beyond a small group of perpetual peace activists to a broader public.

With peace movements, it is clear that threat of war helps organizers mobilize people. Threats generally help political opposition grow beyond conventional politics. Movements against nuclear armaments, for example, emerge strongly when governments announce they are building more weapons. Similarly, environmental movements expand when government policies toward forests, pesticides, or toxic wastes become visibly negligent. In the case of abortion politics, each side has kept the other mobilized for more than 30 years by periodically threatening to take control of the issue. In each of these cases, those who lose in traditional political contests such as elections or lobbying campaigns often take to the streets.

Other sorts of movements grow when the promise of success arises. American civil rights activists, for example, were able to mobilize most broadly when they saw signals that substantial change was possible. Rosa Parks knew about Jackie Robinson and *Brown v. Board of Education*—as well as Gandhian civil disobedience—before deciding not to move to the back of the bus in Montgomery, Alabama. Government responsiveness to earlier activism—such as President Truman's desegregation of the armed forces and calling for an anti-lynching law—though limited, fitful, and often strategic, for a time encouraged others in their efforts. And the success of African-American activists encouraged other ethnic groups, as well as women, to pursue social change through movement politics.

As social movements grow, they incorporate more groups with a broader range of goals and more diverse tactics. Absent a focus like an imminent war, activists inside and political figures outside compete with one another to define movement goals and objectives. Political authorities often respond with policy concessions designed to diminish the breadth and depth of a movement. While such tactics can divide a movement, they are also one way of measuring a movement's success.

HOW MOVEMENTS MATTER: PUBLIC POLICY

By uniting, however loosely, a broad range of groups and individuals, and taking action, social movements can influence public policy, at least by bringing attention to their issues. Newspaper stories about a demonstration pique political, journalistic and public interest in the demonstrators' concerns. By bringing scrutiny to a contested policy, activists can promote alternative thinking. By displaying a large and engaged constituency, social movements provide political support for leaders sympathetic to their concerns. Large demonstrations show that there are passionate citizens who might also donate money, work in campaigns, and vote for candidates who will speak for them. Citizen mobilization against abortion, taxes, and immigration, for example, has encouraged ambitious politicians to cater to those constituencies. In these ways, social movement activism spurs and supports more conventional political action.

Activism outside of government can also strengthen advocates of minority positions within government. Social movements—just like presidential administrations and congressional majorities—are coalitions. Anti-war activists in the streets may have strengthened the bargaining position of the more internationalist factions in the Bush administration, most notably Colin Powell, and led, at least temporarily, to diplomatic action in the United Nations. Mobilized opposition also, for a time, seemed to embolden Congressional critics, and encouraged lesser-known candidates for the Democratic presidential nomination to vocally oppose the war.

Social movements, by the popularity of their arguments, or more frequently the strength of their support, can convince authorities to re-examine and possibly change their policy preferences. Movements can demand a litmus test for their support. Thus, George H. W. Bush, seeking the Republican nomination for president in 1980, revised his prior support for abortion rights. A few years later Jesse Jackson likewise reconsidered his opposition to abortion. Movements raised the profile of the issue, forcing politicians not only to address their concerns, but to accede to their demands.

Although movement activists promote specific policies—a nuclear freeze, an equal rights amendment, an end to legal abortion, or, more recently, a cap on malpractice awards—their demands are usually so absolute that they do not translate well into policy. Indeed, the clearest message that activists can generally send is absolute rejection: no to nuclear weapons, abortion, pesticides or taxes. These admonitions rarely become policy, but by promoting their programs in stark moral terms, activists place the onus on others to offer alternative policies that are, depending on one's perspective, more moderate or complex. At the same time, politicians often use such alternatives to capture, or at least defuse, social movements. The anti-nuclear weapons movement of the late 1950s and early 1960s did not end the arms race or all nuclear testing. It did, however lead to the Limited Test Ban Treaty, which ended atmospheric testing. First Eisenhower then Kennedy, offered arms control proposals and talks with the Soviet Union, at least in part as a response to the movement. This peace movement established the framework for arms control in superpower relations, which subsequently spread to the entire international community.

In these ways, activists shape events—even if they do not necessarily get credit for their efforts or achieve everything they want. The movement against the Vietnam War, for instance, generated a great deal of attention which, in turn, changed the conduct of that war and much else in domestic politics. President Johnson chose bombing targets with attention to minimizing political opposition;

President Nixon, elected at least partly as a result of the backlash against the anti-war movement nonetheless tailored his military strategy to respond to some of its concerns. In later years, he suggested that the anti-war movement made it unthinkable for him to threaten nuclear escalation in Vietnam—even as a bluff. In addition, the movement helped end the draft, institutionalizing all-volunteer armed forces. And, according to Colin Powell, the Vietnam dissenters provoked a new military approach for the United States, one that emphasized the use of overwhelming force to minimize American casualties. Thus, the military execution of the 1991 Persian Gulf war was influenced by an anti-war movement that peaked more than three decades earlier. This is significant, if not the effect most anti-war activists envisioned.

POLITICAL INSTITUTIONS

Social movements can alter not only the substance of policy, but also how policy is made. It is not uncommon for governments to create new institutions, such as departments and agencies, in response to activists' demands. For example, President Kennedy responded to the nuclear freeze movement by establishing the Arms Control and Disarmament Agency, which became a permanent voice and venue in the federal bureaucracy for arms control. A glance at any organizational chart of federal offices turns up numerous departments, boards, and commissions that trace their origins to popular mobilization. These include the Department of Labor, the Department of Housing and Urban Development, the National Labor Relations Board, the Environmental Protection Agency, the National Council on Disability, the Consumer Product Safety Commission and the Equal Employment Opportunity Commission. Although these offices do not always support activist goals, their very existence represents a permanent institutional concern and a venue for making demands. If, as environmentalists argue, the current Environmental Protection Agency is often more interested in facilitating exploitation of the environment than in preventing it, this does not negate the fact that the environmental movement established a set of procedures through which environmental concerns can be addressed.

Government responses to movement demands also include ensuring that diverse voices are heard in decision making. In local zoning decisions, for example, environmental impact statements are a now a routine part of getting a permit for construction. Congress passed legislation establishing this requirement in 1970 in response to the growing environmental movement. Indeed, movement groups, including Greenpeace and the Sierra Club, negotiated directly with congressional sponsors. Similarly, juries and judges now routinely hear victim impact statements before pronouncing sentences in criminal cases, the product of the victims' rights movement. Both public and private organizations have created new departments to manage and, perhaps more importantly document personnel practices, such as hiring and firing, to avoid being sued for discrimination on the basis of gender, ethnicity or disability. Workshops on diversity, tolerance, and sexual harassment are commonplace in American universities and corporations, a change over just two decades that would have been impossible to imagine without the activism of the 1950s and 1960s. In such now well-established bureaucratic routines, we can see how social movements change practices, and through them, beliefs.

Social movements also spawn dedicated organizations that generally survive long after a movement's moment has passed. The environmental movement, for example, firmly established a "big ten" group of national organizations, such as the Wildlife Defense Fund, which survives primarily by raising money from self-defined environmentalists. It cultivates donors by monitoring and publicizing government actions and environmental conditions, lobbying elected officials and administrators, and occasionally mobilizing supporters to do something more than mail in their annual membership renewals. Here, too, the seemingly permanent establishment of "movement organizations" in Washington, D.C. and in state capitals across the United States has—even if these groups often lose—fundamentally changed policymaking. Salaried officers of the organizations routinely screen high-level appointees to the judiciary and government bureaucracy and testify before legislatures. Mindful of this process, policymakers seek to preempt their arguments by modifying policy—or at least their rhetoric.

POLITICAL ACTIVISTS

Social movements also change the people who participate in them, educating as well as mobilizing activists, and thereby promoting ongoing awareness and action that extends beyond the boundaries of one movement or campaign. Those who turn out at anti-war demonstrations today have often cut their activist teeth mobilizing against globalization, on behalf of labor, for animal rights or against welfare reform. By politicizing communities, connecting people, and promoting personal loyalties, social movements build the infrastructure not only of subsequent movements, but of a democratic society more generally.

Importantly these consequences are often indirect and difficult to document. When hundreds of thousands of activists march to the Supreme Court to demonstrate their support for legal abortion, their efforts might persuade a justice. More likely, the march signals commitment and passion to other activists and inspires them to return home and advocate for abortion rights in their communities across the country, thereby affecting the shape of politics and culture more broadly.

The 2003 anti-Iraq War movement mobilized faster, with better organizational ties in the United States and transnationally, than, for example, the movement against the 1991 Persian Gulf War. But how are we to assess its influence? Many activists no doubt see their efforts as having been wasted, or at least as unsuccessful. Moreover, supporters of the war point to the rapid seizure of Baghdad and ouster of Saddam Hussein's regime as evidence of the peace movement's naivete. But a movement's legacy extends through a range of outcomes beyond a government's decision of the moment. It includes consequences for process, institutional practices, organizations and individuals. This anti-war movement changed the rhetoric and international politics of the United States' preparation for war, leading to a detour through the United Nations that delayed the start of war. The activists who marched in Washington, San Francisco and Los Angeles may retreat for awhile, but they are likely to be engaged in politics more intensively in the future. This may not be much consolation to people who marched to stop a war, but it is true. To paraphrase a famous scholar: activists make history, but they do not make it just as they please. In fighting one political battle, they shape the conditions of the next one.

The Problem Is Civil Obedience

HOWARD ZINN

By the latter part of May, 1970, feelings about the war in Vietnam had become almost unbearably intense. In Boston, about a hundred of us decided to sit down at the Boston Army Base and block the road used by buses carrying draftees off to military duty. We were not so daft that we thought we were stopping the flow of soldiers to Vietnam; it was a symbolic act, a statement, a piece of guerrilla theater. We were all arrested and charged, in the quaint language of an old statute, with "sauntering and loitering" in such a way as to obstruct traffic. Eight of us refused to plead guilty, insisting on trial by jury, hoping we could persuade the members of the jury that ours was a justified act of civil disobedience. We did not persuade them. We were found guilty, chose jail instead of paying a fine, but the judge, apparently reluctant to have us in jail, gave us forty-eight hours to change our minds, after which we should show up in court to either pay the fine or be jailed. In the meantime, I had been invited to go to Johns Hopkins University to debate with the philosopher Charles Frankel on the issue of civil disobedience. I decided it would be hypocritical for me, an advocate of civil disobedience, to submit dutifully to the court and thereby skip out on an opportunity to speak to hundreds of students about civil disobedience. So, on the day I was supposed to show up in court in Boston I flew to Baltimore and that evening debated with Charles Frankel. Returning to Boston I decided to meet my morning class, but two detectives were waiting for me, and I was hustled before the court and then spent a couple of days in jail. What follows is the transcript of my opening statement in the debate at Johns Hopkins. It was included in a book published by Johns Hopkins Press in 1972, entitled *Violence: The Crisis of American Confidence.*

I start from the supposition that the world is topsy-turvy, that things are all wrong, that the wrong people are in jail and the wrong people are out of jail, that the wrong people are in power and the wrong people are out of power, that the wealth is distributed in this country and the world in such a way as not simply

Source: "The Problem Is Civil Obedience" by Howard Zinn from *The Zinn Reader,* 1997. Reprinted by permission of Seven Stories Press.

to require small reform but to require a drastic reallocation of wealth. I start from the supposition that we don't have to say too much about this because all we have to do is think about the state of the world today and realize that things are all upside down. Daniel Berrigan is in jail—a Catholic priest, a poet who opposes the war—and J. Edgar Hoover is free, you see. David Dellinger, who has opposed war ever since he was this high and who has used all of his energy and passion against it, is in danger of going to jail. The men who are responsible for the My Lai massacre are not on trial; they are in Washington serving various functions, primary and subordinate, that have to do with the unleashing of massacres, which surprise them when they occur. At Kent State University four students were killed by the National Guard and students were indicted. In every city in this country, when demonstrations take place, the protestors, whether they have demonstrated or not, whatever they have done, are assaulted and clubbed by police, and then they are arrested for assaulting a police officer.

Now, I have been studying very closely what happens every day in the courts in Boston, Massachusetts. You would be astounded—maybe you wouldn't, maybe you have been around, maybe you have lived maybe you have thought, maybe you have been hit—at how the daily rounds of injustice make their way through this marvelous thing that we call due process. Well, that is my premise.

All you have to do is read the Soledad letters of George Jackson, who was sentenced to one year to life, of which he spent ten years, for a seventy-dollar robbery of a filling station. And then there is the U.S. Senator who is alleged to keep 185,000 dollars a year, or something like that, on the oil depletion allowance. One is theft; the other is legislation. Something is wrong, something is terribly wrong when we ship 10,000 bombs full of nerve gas across the country, and drop them in somebody else's swimming pool so as not to trouble our own. So you lose your perspective after a while. If you don't think, if you just listen to TV and read scholarly things, you actually begin to think that things are not so bad, or that just little things are wrong. But you have to get a little detached, and then come back and look at the world, and you are horrified. So we have to start from that supposition—that things are really topsy-turvy.

And our topic is topsy-turvy: civil disobedience. As soon as you say the topic is civil disobedience, you are saying our *problem* is civil disobedience. That is *not* our problem. . . . Our problem is civil *obedience*. Our problem is the numbers of people all over the world who have obeyed the dictates of the leaders of their government and have gone to war, and millions have been killed because of this obedience. And our problem is that scene in *All Quiet on the Western Front* where the schoolboys march off dutifully in a line to war. Our problem is that people are obedient all over the world, in the face of poverty and starvation and stupidity; and war and cruelty. Our problem is that people are obedient while the jails are full of petty thieves, and all the while the grand thieves are running the country. That's our problem. We recognize this for Nazi Germany. We know that the problem there was obedience, that the people obeyed Hitler. People obeyed; that was wrong. They should have challenged, and they should have resisted; and if we were only there, we would have showed them. Even in Stalin's Russia we can understand that; people are obedient, all these herdlike people.

But America is different. That is what we've all been brought up on. From the time we are this high—and I still hear it resounding in Mr. Frankel's statement—you tick off; one, two, three, four, five lovely things about America that we don't want disturbed very much.

But if we have learned anything in the past ten years, it is that these lovely things about America were never lovely. We have been expansionist and aggressive and mean to other people from the beginning. And we're aggressive and mean to people in this country, and we've allocated the wealth of this country in a very unjust way. We've never had justice in the courts for the poor people, for black people, for radicals. Now how can we boast that America is a very special place? It is not that special. It really isn't.

Well, that is our topic, that is our problem: civil obedience. Law is very important. We are talking about obedience to law—law, this marvelous invention of modern times, which we attribute to Western civilization, and which we talk about proudly. The rule of law, oh, how wonderful, all these courses in Western civilization all over the land. Remember those bad old days when people were exploited by feudalism? Everything was terrible in the Middle Ages—but now we have Western civilization, the rule of law. *The rule of law has regularized and maximized the injustice that existed before the rule of law, that is what the rule of law has done.* Let us start looking at the rule of law realistically, not with that metaphysical complacency with which we always examined it before.

When in all the nations of the world the rule of law is the darling of the leaders and the plague of the people, we ought to begin to recognize this. We have to transcend these national boundaries in our thinking. Nixon and Brezhnev have much more in common with one another than we have with Nixon. J. Edgar Hoover has far more in common with the head of the Soviet secret police than he has with us. It's the international dedication to law and order that binds the leaders of all countries in a comradely bond. That's why we are always surprised when they get together they smile, they shake hands, they smoke cigars, they really like one another no matter what they say. It's like the Republican and Democratic parties, who claim that it's going to make a terrible difference if one or the other wins, yet they are all the same. Basically, it is us against them.

Yossarian was right, remember, in *Catch-22*? He had been accused of giving aid and comfort to the enemy, which nobody should ever be accused of, and Yossarian said to his friend Clevinger: "The enemy is whoever is going to get you killed, whichever side they are on." But that didn't sink in, so he said to Clevinger: "Now you remember that, or one of these days you'll be dead." And remember? Clevinger, after a while, was dead. And we must remember that our enemies are not divided along national lines, that enemies are not just people who speak different languages and occupy different territories. Enemies are people who want to get us killed.

We are asked, "What if everyone disobeyed the law?" But a better question is, "what if everyone obeyed the law?" And the answer to the question is much easier to come by, because we have a lot of empirical evidence about what happens if everyone obeys the law, or if even most people obey the law. What happens is what has happened, what is happening. Why do people revere the law? And we all do; even I have to fight it, for it was put into my bones at an early age when I was a Cub Scout. One reason we revere the law is its ambivalence. In the modern world we deal with phrases and words that have multiple meanings, like "national security." Oh, yes, we must do this for national security! Well, what does that mean? Whose national security? Where? When? Why? We don't bother to answer those questions, or even to ask them.

The law conceals many things. The law is the Bill of Rights. In fact, that is what we think of when we develop our reverence for the law. The law is something that protects us; the law is our right—the law is the Constitution. Bill of Rights Day, essay contests sponsored by the American Legion on our Bill of Rights, that is the law. And that is good.

But there is another part of the law that doesn't get ballyhooed—the legislation that has gone through month after month, year after year, from the beginning of the Republic, which allocates the resources of the country in such a way as to leave some people very rich and other people very poor; and still others scrambling like mad for what little is left. That is the law. If you go to law school you will see this. You can quantify it by counting the big, heavy law books that people carry around with them and see how many law books you count that say "Constitutional Rights" on them and how many that say "Property," "Contracts," "Torts," "Corporation Law." That is what the law is mostly about. The law is the oil depletion allowance—although we don't have Oil Depletion Allowance Day, we don't have essays written on behalf of the oil depletion allowance. So there are parts of the law that are publicized and played up to us—oh, this is the law, the Bill of Rights. And there are other parts of the law that just do their quiet work, and nobody says anything about them.

It started way back. When the Bill of Rights was first passed, remember, in the first administration of Washington? Great thing. Bill of Rights passed! Big ballyhoo. At the same time Hamilton's economic program was passed. Nice, quiet, money to the rich—I'm simplifying it a little, but not too much. Hamilton's economic program started it off. You can draw a straight line from Hamilton's economic program to the oil depletion allowance to the tax write-offs for corporations. All the way through—that is the history. The Bill of Rights publicized; economic legislation unpublicized.

You know the enforcement of different parts of the law is as important as the publicity attached to the different parts of the law. The Bill of Rights, is it enforced? Not very well. You'll find that freedom of speech in constitutional law is a very difficult, ambiguous, troubled concept. Nobody really knows when you can get up and speak and when you can't. Just check all of the Supreme Court decisions. Talk about predictability in a system—you can't predict what will happen to you when you get up on the street corner and speak. See if you can tell the difference between the *Terminiello* case and the *Feiner* case, and see if you can figure out what is going to happen. By the way, there is one part of the law that is not very vague, and that involves the right to distribute leaflets on the street. The Supreme Court has been very clear on that. In decision after decision we are affirmed an absolute right to distribute leaflets on the street. Try it. Just go out on the street and start distributing leaflets. And a policeman comes up to you and he says, "Get out of here." And you say, "Aha! Do you know *Marsh v. Alabama*, 1946?" That is the reality of the Bill of Rights. That's the reality of the Constitution, that part of the law which is portrayed to us as a beautiful and marvelous thing. And seven years after the Bill of Rights was passed, which said that "Congress shall make no law abridging the freedom of speech," Congress made a law abridging the freedom of speech. Remember? The Sedition Act of 1798.

So the Bill of Rights was not enforced. Hamilton's program was enforced, because when the whisky farmers went out and rebelled you remember, in 1794 in Pennsylvania, Hamilton himself got on his horse and went out there to suppress the rebellion to make sure that the revenue tax was enforced. And you can trace the story right down to the present day, what laws are enforced, what laws are not enforced. So you have to be careful when you say, "I'm for the law, I revere the law." What part of the law are you talking about? I'm not against all law. But I think we ought to begin to make very important distinctions about what laws do what things to what people.

And there are other problems with the law. It's a strange thing, we think that law brings order. Law doesn't. How do we know that law does not bring order? Look around us. We live under the rules of law. Notice how much order we have? People say we have to worry about civil disobedience because it will lead to anarchy. Take a look at the present world in which the rule of law obtains. This is the closest to what is called anarchy in the popular mind—confusion, chaos, international banditry. The only order that is really worth anything does not come through the enforcement of law, it comes through the establishment of a society which is just and in which harmonious relationships are established and in which you need a minimum of regulation to create decent sets of arrangements among people. But the order based on law and on the *force* of law is the order of the totalitarian state, and it inevitably leads either to total injustice or to rebellion—eventually, in other words, to very great disorder.

We all grow up with the notion that the law is holy. They asked Daniel Berrigan's mother what she thought of her son's breaking the law. He burned draft records—one of the most violent acts of this century—to protest the war, for which he was sentenced to prison, as criminals should be. They asked his mother who is in her eighties, what she thought of her son's breaking the law. And she looked straight into the interviewer's face, and she said, "It's not God's law." Now we forget that. There is nothing sacred about the law. Think of who makes laws. The law is not made by God, it is made by Strom Thurmond. If you have any notion about the sanctity and loveliness and reverence for the law, look at the legislators around the country who make the laws. Sit in on the sessions of the state legislatures. Sit in on Congress, for these are the people who make the laws which we are then supposed to revere.

All this is done with such propriety as to fool us. This is the problem. In the old days, things were confused; you didn't know. Now you know. It is all down there in the books. Now we go through due process. Now the same things happen as happened before, except that we've gone through the right procedures. In Boston a policeman walked into a hospital ward and fired five times at a black man who had snapped a towel at his arm—and killed him. A hearing was held. The judge decided that the policeman was justified because if he didn't do it, he would lose the respect of his fellow officers. Well, that is what is known as due process—that is, the guy didn't get away with it. We went through the proper procedures, and everything was set up. The decorum, the propriety of the law fools us.

The nation then, was founded on disrespect for the law, and then came the Constitution and the notion of stability which Madison and Hamilton liked. But then we found in certain crucial times in our history that the legal framework did not suffice, and in order to end Slavery we had to go outside the legal framework, as we had to do at the time of the American Revolution or the Civil War. The union had to go outside the legal framework in order to establish certain rights in the 1930s. And in this time, which may be more critical than the Revolution or the Civil War, the problems are so horrendous as to require us to go outside the legal framework in order to make a statement, to resist, to begin to establish the kind of institutions and relationships which a decent society should have. No, not just tearing things down; building things up. But even if you build things up that you are not supposed to build up—you try to build up a people's park, that's not tearing down a system; you are building something up, but you are doing it illegally—the militia comes in and drives you out. That is the form that civil disobedience is going to take more and more, people trying to build a new society in the midst of the old.

But what about voting and elections? Civil disobedience—we don't need that much of it, we are told, because we can go through the electoral system. And by now we should have learned, but maybe we haven't, for we grew up with the notion that the voting booth is a sacred place, almost like a confessional. You walk into the voting booth and you come out and they snap your picture and then put it in the papers with a beatific smile on your face. You've just voted; that is democracy. But if you even read what the political scientists say—although who can?—about the voting process, you find that the voting process is a sham. Totalitarian states love voting. You get people to the polls and they register their approval. I know there is a difference—they have one party and we have two parties. We have one more party than they have, you see.

What we are trying to do, I assume, is really to get back to the principles and aims and spirit of the Declaration of Independence. This spirit is resistance to illegitimate authority and to forces that deprive people of their life and liberty and right to pursue happiness, and therefore under these conditions, it urges the right to alter or abolish their current form of government—and the stress had been on abolish. But to establish the principles of the Declaration of Independence, we are going to need to go outside the law, to stop obeying the laws that demand killing or that allocate wealth the way it has been done, or that put people in jail for petty technical offenses and keep other people our of jail for enormous crimes. My hope is that this kind of spirit will take place not just in this country but in other countries because they all need it. People in all countries need the spirit of disobedience to the state, which is not a metaphysical thing but a thing of force and wealth. And we need a kind of declaration of interdependence among people in all countries of the world who are striving for the same thing.

_____ ADDITIONAL READINGS_____

Arkin, William M. 2003. "The Dividends of Delay." _Los Angeles Times_ (February 23) M1.

Arkin details the influence of the peace movement on U.S. military strategy in the Iraq War.

Giugni, Marco, Doug McAdam, and Charles Tilly. 1999. _How Social Movements Matter._ Minneapolis, MN: University at Minnesota Press.

This collection employs diverse approaches in examining the outcomes of social movements across a range of cases.

Meyer, David S., Nancy Whittier, and Belinda Robnett (eds.). 2002. _Social Movements: Identity Culture, and the State._ New York: Oxford University Press.

A collection that addresses the link between protesters and context across different settings and times.

Rochon, Thomas. _Culture Moves: Ideas, Activism, and Changing Values._ 1998. Princeton, NJ: Princeton University Press.

Rochon looks at social movements as a primary way to promote new ideas and alter culture.

Zinn, Howard. _A People's History of the United States, 1492–Present._ 2003. New York: Perennial Classics.

Zinn writes a bottom-up history of the United States that features the contributions of social movements and activists to the progress of the nation across time.

CHAPTER 2

Social Movements Advancing toward Equality

Certain categories of people experience discrimination, negative stereotypes, and powerlessness because they differ from the dominant groups in terms of economic resources, racial classification, gender, sexual orientation, and because of physical, sensory, or cognitive impairments. This chapter examines social movements that seek to reduce inequities by class, race, gender, sexuality, or disability.

Although many of these types of movements originated long ago, a take-off period for their effectiveness was roughly from 1955 through 1975. During these turbulent times a key catalyst for social equality movements was the civil rights struggle. Considered by the majority at the time as being radical, subversive, and dangerous, the long-run achievements of this movement resulted in:

- The breakdown of the 100-year-old system of Jim Crow segregation in the South
- Landmark civil rights legislation featuring the Civil Rights Act of 1964 and Voting Rights Act of 1965
- President Lyndon Johnson's Great Society program instituting the war on poverty

The first selection in this chapter recalls the context and spirit of the civil rights movement by describing a key confrontation that expanded the well-known struggle by Martin Luther King, Jr., to desegregate public facilities such as transportation and schools in the South. On February 1, 1960, four black freshmen students from North Carolina A & T State University ordered meals at the whites-only lunch counter at the Woolworth Store in downtown Greensboro. They changed history because their action challenged segregation policies followed by private businesses. Two days later, students occupied sixty-three of the sixty-five seats available at the same Woolworth's lunch counter, and just two months later the sit-in movement had spread to fifty-four cities in nine states.

Acts like this student sit-in and the previously mentioned action by Rosa Parks that started the public bus system boycott in Montgomery, Alabama, inspired numerous other groups to stand up for equality in the 1960s, 1970s, and afterward. In the second reading for this chapter, author Charles Wilson recounts

"Rosa Parks's Gift to the Disabled" by tracing the link between her act of courage and the disability rights movement that has since resulted in the Americans with Disabilities Act of 1990 (ADA), which did much to improve equal access and participation for Americans with disabilities in mainstream society.

Other equality movements that took off from the civil rights struggle include the women's movement and the struggle for gay rights. Our third and fourth selections for this chapter elaborate these connections. Tina Gianoulis shows how the women's movement pre-dated the civil rights movement, but also was lifted to new levels because of it. Similarly, the fourth article reveals the prior roots of the gay rights movement and shows how it was energized by the social impacts of the civil rights activists.

The civil rights movement of the 1950s through the 1970s had enormous impact on matters of equality in America. Its stellar achievements inspired others to struggle from the bottom up to work toward greater equality for disabled Americans, women, and gays, among others. Ironically, though, the direct objectives of the civil rights struggle still remain to be fully achieved. From the beginning, the civil rights movement sought to solve the social problems of discrimination against people of color and poverty. Our final reading focuses on one current legacy of this cause.

The Living Wage Movement is spearheaded by the Association of Community Organizations for Reform Now (ACORN). Today one of its core goals is to help the working poor receive wages equal to or exceeding the poverty line for a family of four (currently estimated at $9.06 an hour). According to census data, over 2.9 million full-time workers were below the poverty line in 2004 (U.S. Bureau of the Census, 2005:10). Despite working, these people remained poor because they held menial, dead-end jobs that had no benefits, and were paid the minimum wage or below. The federal minimum wage of $5.15 adds up to $10,712 per year for full-time work. The poverty line for a family of four in 2004 was $19,157, so the deficit for a full-time minimum wage worker was $8,454. ACORN is now the nation's oldest and largest grassroots organization of low and moderate income people with over 150,000 member families organized into 800 neighborhood chapters in 65 cities. In addition to the living wage campaign, ACORN members organize to promote affordable housing, safety, education, improved city services, tenant rights, and fair banking and insurance practices for poor and middle-class Americans (ACORN, 2003). The origins and objectives of ACORN's Living Wage Movement are detailed in the closing article for this chapter.

REFERENCES

ACORN. 2003. "Introduction to ACORN's Living Wage Web Site." Brooklyn, NY: Living Wage Resource Center. www.livingwagecampaign.org.

U.S. Bureau of the Census. 2005. "Income, Poverty, and Health Insurance Coverage in the United States: 2004." *Current Population Reports*, P60-229 (August).

The Sit-In Movement

TAYLOR BRANCH

Monday, February 1, students at the Negro colleges around Greensboro, North Carolina, were electrified by reports of what four freshman boys had done that day. Even the words that had started it all were the stuff of new myth. At a bull session, one of them had said, "We might as well go now." Another had replied, "You really mean it?" The first had said, "Sure, I mean it," and the four of them had gone to the downtown Woolworth's store and slipped into seats at the sacrosanct whites-only lunch counter. The Negro waitress had said, "Fellows like you make our race look bad," and refused to serve them, but the four freshmen had not only sat there unperturbed all afternoon but also promised to return at ten o'clock the next morning to continue what they called a "sit-down protest." That night, the four instantly famous students on the campus of North Carolina A&T were meeting with elected student leaders, and rumors spread that others were volunteering to join them in the morning. With telephones buzzing between campuses, word flashed that even some white students from Greensboro College wanted to sit in with them. The student leaders were arranging it so that students could sit down in shifts so as not to miss classes. Nineteen students sat with the four freshmen at Woolworth's on Tuesday. On Wednesday, the number swelled to eighty-five as the "sit-in" became a contagion.

No one had time to wonder why the Greensboro sit-in was so different. In the previous three years, similar demonstrations had occurred in at least sixteen other cities. Few of them made the news, all faded quickly from public notice, and none had the slightest catalytic effect anywhere else. By contrast, Greensboro helped define the new decade. Almost certainly, the lack of planning helped create the initial euphoria. Because the four students at Woolworth's had no plan, they began with no self-imposed limitations. They defined no tactical goals. They did not train or drill in preparation. They did not dwell on the many forces that might he used against them. Above all, they did not anticipate that Woolworth's

Source: Reprinted and abridged with the permission of Simon & Schuster Adult Publishing Group, from *Parting the Waters: America in the King Years 1954–1963* by Taylor Branch (pp. 271–275, 278–280). Copyright © 1988 by Taylor Branch. All rights reserved.

white managers would—instead of threatening to have them arrested—flounder in confusion and embarrassment. The surprise discovery of defensiveness within the segregated white world turned their fear into elation.

The spontaneity and open-endedness of the first Greensboro sit-in flashed through the network of activists who had been groping toward the same goal. On the first night, the first four protesters themselves contacted Floyd McKissick, who, as a maverick lawyer and NAACP Youth Council leader, had joined Rev. Douglas Moore in the Durham ice cream parlor case and other small sit-ins. McKissick and Moore rushed to nearby Greensboro. Simultaneously, the news traveled along parallel lines of communication with such speed that a vice president of the mostly white National Student Association was in Greensboro on February 2, the second day, before any word of the sit-in had appeared in the public media.

On the third day, when the number of protesters passed eighty, Douglas Moore called James Lawson in Nashville with a volley of bulletins. The protest would continue to grow, he reported, as enthusiastic student volunteers were only too eager to absorb the organizing discipline of the adults who had arrived to work in the background. The sit-in "command center" at North Carolina A&T was operating with crisp, military efficiency—briefing new protesters on nonviolence, quashing rumors, dispatching fresh troops as needed. Most important, Moore reported, sympathetic sit-ins were about to begin in Durham, Raleigh, and other North Carolina cities. Moore, who knew already that Lawson had been preparing for new Nashville protests, urged him to speed up the schedule so that the movement could spread into other states. Lawson promised to try. Moore then made other calls, including one to the FOR's Glenn Smiley. McKissick called Gordon Carey, the CORE official who had worked on Wyatt Walker's Richmond march and the Miami sit-ins the previous year. Carey flew from New York to Durham at the end of the first week. By Saturday, the Greensboro sit-in counted some four hundred students, and Kress, the other big downtown dime store, had been added to the target list. A bomb scare that day interrupted the demonstrations. Later, Klansmen and youth-gang members crowded inside the stores to menace the protesters. Store managers who had been desperately polite all week now threatened to call in legal force.

Before serious reprisal fell upon Greensboro, fresh sit-ins broke out the following Monday in the surrounding North Carolina cities of Raleigh, Durham, and Winston-Salem. Three days later in nearby High Point, students assembled at a church before marching downtown to the segregated lunch counters, and as it happened, Fred Shuttlesworth had come in from Birmingham to preach the midweek service for the minister of that church. Shuttlesworth became the first eyewitness from the tough Deep South states below North Carolina. He saw the well-dressed students step off in good order, like soldiers in the joyous early stages of a popular war, and he heard that it was the same in the other North

Carolina towns—only bigger. Shuttlesworth promptly called Ella Baker at the SCLC office in Atlanta. He was not the first to report to her about the sit-ins, but he was the first voice of authority from the inner circle of SCLC preachers. This is it, he told Baker. "You must tell Martin that we must get with this," said Shuttlesworth, adding that the sit-ins might "shake up the world."

The movement first leaped across state lines on the day after the High Point sit-in. An SCLC preacher in Rock Hill, South Carolina, reported by phone to McKissick that his charges were "ready to go." They went from his church to the lunch counters on Friday, the same day police arrested forty-one students sitting in at the Cameron Village Woolworth store in Raleigh. In handcuffs, the Raleigh students swept across the threshold of the jail with eyes closed and hearts pounding, and, like the bus boycotters four years earlier, they soon re-emerged on bail to discover that their identities had not been crushed. They were unharmed and did not feel like trash. A flood of relief swelled their enthusiasm.

In Nashville that Friday night, Lawson presided over what turned out to be the first mass meeting of the sit-in movement. About five hundred new volunteers crowded into the First Baptist Church along with the seventy-five veterans of the nonviolence workshop. Lawson and the other adults argued for delay, on the grounds that only a small fraction of the students had received any training. This was not a game, they said. Sooner or later the city would put demonstrators in jail, and their organization—the Nashville Christian Leadership Conference, a local affiliate of King's SCLC—had less than $100 in reserve. They needed time to raise a bail fund. These and other words of caution gave way to a tide of student sentiment, however, and Lawson found himself giving a crash course on nonviolence late into the night. He told the crowd how to behave in the face of a hundred possible emergencies, how to avoid violating the loitering laws, how to move to and from the lunch counters in orderly shifts, how to fill the seats of students who needed to go to the bathroom, even how to dress: stockings and heels for the women, coats and ties for the fellows. When in doubt, he stressed, the newcomers should take their cue from the behavior of the workshop members who had demonstrated before.

They broke up that night amid nervous prayers and whispers of "Good luck," and Lawson's logistical plan worked smoothly the next morning. Church cars traveled a circuit between the First Baptist Church and designated pickup spots near Nashville's four Negro colleges—Fisk University, Tennessee State, Meharry Medical, and the Baptist seminary. When all were assembled at the First Baptist staging area, Lawson moved them out five hundred strong. White Nashville, which had changed hands nearly a dozen times during the Civil War, awoke slowly to a kind of invasion force it never had encountered before, as rows of neatly dressed Negro college students filed into the downtown stores to wait for food service.

The Nashville students—destined to establish themselves as the largest, most disciplined, and most persistent of the nonviolent action groups in the South—extended the sit-in movement into its third state. Their success helped form the model of the student group—recruited from the campuses, quartered in the churches, and advised by preachers. Elated with the early results, Lawson called King, Ella Baker, and Douglas Moore, among others, to exchange reports. Each of them in turn called acquaintances who might help open other fronts. By the end of February, sit-in campaigns were under way in thirty-one Southern cities across eight states. News attention remained scanty for the most part in both white and Negro media, largely because people were conditioned to think of student antics as transient events. Moore predicted that the sit-ins soon would put an end to such complacency. "If Woolworth and the other stores think this is just another panty raid," he told reporters, "they haven't had their sociologists in the field recently." . . .

In Nashville, the students in Lawson's workshop had completed their second week of daily sit-ins on Friday, February 26, when the chief of police let it be known that their grace period was over. He warned that the downtown merchants had requested trespassing or disorderly conduct arrests if the demonstrations continued. This was the challenge for which the students had braced themselves. John Lewis stayed up all night composing a list of nonviolent "do's and don'ts" to guide the students through the trauma of being arrested. The secretary to the seminary's president typed them on a mimeograph stencil, ending with Lewis' earnest admonition: "Remember the teachings of Jesus, Gandhi, Thoreau, and Martin Luther King, Jr."

Each student carried one of the mimeographed sheets the next day as the column marched silently back downtown to the designated stores. Hostile white teenagers shouted "Chicken" and "Nigger." The police allowed some of the whites to attack Lawson's unresisting troops with rocks, fists, and lighted cigarettes before moving in to arrest seventy-seven Negroes and five white sympathizers—to the applause of several hundred white onlookers. When a policeman said "You're under arrest" to John Lewis, a lifetime of absorbed taboos against any kind of trouble with the law quickened into terror. He tried to blot out everything but his rules as the police frisked, cuffed, and marched him to the paddy wagon. Then, riding to jail with the others, his dread gave way to an exhilaration unlike any he had ever known. They had held steady through the worst, he believed, and by the highest standards they knew there was no doubt that they had been in the right. Their fervor rose to such heights that Lewis and some of the other workshop veterans made a pact that weekend to escalate their Gandhian witness.

At their trials on Monday, the twenty-ninth, their chosen speaker, stood up in court to interrupt the monotonous drone of guilty verdicts and fines. Diane Nash—a Chicago native as dedicated as Lewis and much more articulate—

informed the judge that a group of the defendants had decided to choose jail instead of a fine. "We feel that if we pay these fines we would be contributing to and supporting the injustice and immoral practices that have been performed in the arrest and conviction of the defendants," she announced nervously. Nash, Lewis, and fourteen others were soon led off to jail, making good on the Gandhian gesture King himself had tried unsuccessfully in Montgomery a year and a half earlier. The emotional force of their example was so strong that more than sixty of their fellow defendants changed their minds, pocketed their fine money, and joined them in jail. Outside the courtroom, many Negroes were shocked at the news that their city, forced to choose, had imprisoned some of the finest students in the area instead of the white hoodlums who had attacked them. Some also felt shame at remaining aloof from the protests while such treatment was being meted out to the nonviolent students. Among those most deeply affected was James Bevel, who came down from his bathroom soliloquies to lead the next wave of demonstrators by the same route to jail, where he was greeted by an overjoyed John Lewis.

The spectacle of the sit-ins had worked the critical degree of conversion in Bevel, and similar changes spread so rapidly through an aroused Negro population that Mayor Ben West made a conciliatory move. In exchange for a halt in the demonstrations, he offered to release the jailed students and appoint a biracial committee to make recommendations about segregation at downtown stores. Nash, Lewis, Bevel, and the other students emerged from jail as heroes who had forced a Southern city to grant one of the long-denied requests of the established civil rights groups. Hard upon the news of this victory, however, came the news that the trustees of Vanderbilt University had summarily expelled James Lawson from the Divinity School without a hearing or the approval of the faculty. The expulsion was reported on the front page of *The New York Times,* beginning national coverage of the onrushing clash between the university and the Vanderbilt faculty. About four hundred Vanderbilt teachers came to resign in protest, ultimately forcing Lawson's reinstatement. Meanwhile, the intrepid Diane Nash led a band of protesters to the lunch counter at the Greyhound bus terminal, which was not covered by the truce with the mayor. There, to the surprise of the entire city, the management served the students without incident. Segregation was broken at Greyhound even as the Vanderbilt trustees were counterattacking against Lawson. The pattern of the early sit-ins was established: constant surprises, all-night meetings, serial victories, and setbacks, with the elders of both races often on the defensive against their young.

Rosa Parks's Gift to the Disabled

CHARLES WILSON

On an unseasonably warm September day in 1984, about a dozen men and women rolled their wheelchairs in front of a city bus that was pulling onto State Street in Chicago. Then they sat there and didn't move. The group had no secret agenda; they simply wanted to make a point. Days before, the Chicago Transit Authority had announced that it was purchasing 363 new public buses— and that none of them would be equipped with wheelchair lifts to serve disabled passengers because the lifts had been deemed too expensive. This ragtag group of wheelchair riders, who were affiliated with a disability rights organization called ADAPT, or Americans Disabled for Accessible Public Transit, decided to protest that decision by obstructing a bus until the police carted them away. Every one of them wore a simple paper name tag, the sort that you would normally see at a meet-and-greet. They all said: "My name is Rosa Parks."

Rosa Parks's act of courage in Montgomery, Ala., in 1955 did more than dismantle the system of racial segregation on public transportation. Her refusal to give up her seat to a white man also created a legacy she never could have foreseen. It was through Parks's example that the disabled community transformed its own often disorganized cause into a unified disability rights movement. "Had it not been for Parks and the bus boycott, there is no question that the disability rights movement would have been light-years behind, if it would have ever occurred," says Michael. Auberger, a disability rights activist who was one of the first to place his wheelchair in front of a bus in the early 1980s. "Her genius was that she saw the bus as the great integrator: It took you to work, it took you to play, it took you to places that you were never before seen. We began to see the bus the same way, too, and it empowered a group of people who had been just as disenfranchised as African Americans."

The disability rights movement could in no sense have been called a movement when Parks refused to yield her seat. At that time, the unemployment rate for people with disabilities reached over 70 percent, and organizations that rallied

Source: "The Other Movement That Rosa Parks Inspired" by Charles Wilson, *The Washington Post,* October 30, 2005, p. B-1. Reprinted by permission of Charles Wilson.

for rights for people with disabilities focused on solutions that were specific to a single disorder. "The disability community was fragmented," says Bob Kafka, a quadriplegic who broke his neck in 1973 and who was an early organizer for ADAPT. "The deaf community wanted interpreters. People with mobility issues wanted curb cuts. The blind wanted more sensory communication. Everyone saw themselves as a deaf person, or a blind person, or a mental health person. We were tossed salad, not fondue."

Parks's action offered these separate communities a strategy that unified their various wishes. "Rosa Parks energized us in that she was the perfect symbol for when the meek become militant," says Kafka. "She was someone who was willing to cross the line." And the fight for accessible public transportation was to be the single issue that catalyzed disparate disability groups into a common cause.

By the 1960s and '70s, many cities had introduced paratransit services that picked up disabled patients. The officials who controlled city budgets, though, typically stipulated that these buses could be used by an individual only a few times a month and that the buses could be used only by appointment. So, in the late '70s and early '80s, some activists began to extend the logic of Parks's silent act of defiance to their own cause: Buses that divided people into separate categories, they said, were inherently unequal. Disabled people shouldn't be limited to using paratransit buses. They deserved to ride the city buses, just like everyone else.

"How could you go to school, or go on a date, or volunteer somewhere if the only trips deemed worth funding for you were medical trips?" wrote ADAPT member Stephanie Thomas in her introduction to "To Ride the Public's Buses," a collection of articles about the early bus actions that appeared in Disability Rag. "How could you get a job if you could only get 3 rides a week? If you were never on time?"

Parks's method of dissent—sitting still—was well suited to a community in which many people found themselves having to do that very thing all day long. Within two decades of her refusal to give up her seat, disabled people in cities across the country began staging their own "sit-ins" by parking their wheelchairs in front of ill-equipped city buses—or, alternatively, by ditching their wheelchairs and crawling onto the stairs of the bus vestibules.

■

Some of the sit-ins were individual acts of defiance. In Hartford, Conn., 63-year-old Edith Harris parked her wheelchair in front of 10 separate local buses on a single day after waiting nearly two hours for an accessible bus. Increasingly, though, the sit-ins were organized by ADAPT and involved many wheelchair users at a single location.

These actions began to change both how disabled people were perceived and how they perceived themselves. "Without the history of Parks and Martin Luther King, the only argument that the disability community had was the Jerry Lewis

Principle," explains Auberger. "The Poor Pathetic Cripple Principle. But if you take a single disabled person and you show them that they can stop a bus, you've empowered that person. And you've made them feel they had rights."

The sit-ins also began to bring about concrete changes in the policies of urban transportation boards. In 1983, the city of Denver gave up its initial resistance and retrofitted all 250 of its buses with lifts after 45 wheelchair users blocked buses at the downtown intersection of Colfax Avenue and Broadway. Similar moves were made by Washington's Metro board in 1986 and by Chicago's transit authority in 1989. And in 1990, when the landmark Americans with Disabilities Act cleared Congress, the only provisions that went into effect immediately were those that mandated accessible public transportation.

If Rosa Parks left a lasting legacy on the disability rights movement, it is important to recognize that it is a legacy that is largely unfinished. A restored version of the bus that Rosa Parks rode in Montgomery recently went on display at the Henry Ford Museum near Detroit, the city where Parks lived her last decades and died Oct. 24 [2005]. Detroit's mayor, Kwame Kilpatrick . . . memorialized Parks by saying that "she stood up by sitting down. I'm only standing here because of her."

Kilpatrick failed to mention a further irony, though: The Justice Department joined a suit against his city in March. It was initially filed in August 2004 by Richard Bernstein, a blind 31-year-old lawyer from the Detroit suburb of Farmington Hills, on behalf of four disabled inner-city clients. His plaintiffs said that they routinely waited three to four hours in severe cold for a bus with a working lift.

Their complaint cited evidence that half of the lifts on the city's bus fleet were routinely broken. The complaint did not ask for compensation. It demanded only that the Motor City comply with the Americans with Disabilities Act. The city recently purchased more accessible buses, but the mayor didn't offer a plan for making sure the buses stayed in good working order. He has publicly disparaged Bernstein on radio as an example of "suburban guys coming into our community trying to raise up the concerns of people when this administration is going to the wall on this issue of disabled riders."

Mayor Kilpatrick is not going to the wall, and neither are many other mayors in this country. A 2002 federal Bureau of Transportation Statistics study found that 6 million Americans with disabilities still have trouble obtaining the transportation they need. Many civic leaders and officials at transit organizations have made arguments about the economic difficulty of installing lifts on buses and maintaining them. But they are seeing only one side of the argument: More people in the disability community would pursue jobs and pay more taxes if they could only trust that they could get to work and back safely.

■

Public officials who have offered elaborate eulogies to Parks's memory in the past two weeks should evaluate whether they are truly living up to the power of her ideas. During a visit to Detroit in August to speak to disabled transit riders for a project I was working on, I met Robert Harvey, who last winter hurled his wheel-chair in front of a bus pulling onto Woodward Avenue after "four drivers in a row had passed him by. (He was knocked to the curb.) I met Carolyn Reed, who has spina bifida and had lost a job because she could rarely find a bus that would get her to work on time. Her able-bodied friends had also recently stopped inviting her to the movies. She guessed why: A few times over the past months, they had found themselves waiting late at night with her for hours to catch a bus with a working lift. "'I'd say, 'Go ahead, go ahead, I'll be all right,'" she told me. "And they'd say, 'We're not leaving you out here.'" I also met Willie Cochran, a double amputee who once waited six hours in freezing temperatures for a bus that would take him home from dialysis treatment.

None of this should be happening in America. "Rosa Parks could get on the bus to protest," says Roger McCarville, a veteran in Detroit who once chained himself to a bus. "We still can't get on the bus." A true tribute to Parks would be to ensure that every American can.

Living the Legacy: The Women's Rights Movement 1848–1998

BONNIE EISENBERG AND MARY RUTHSDOTTER

"Never doubt that a small group of thoughtful, committed citizens can change the world. Indeed, it's the only thing that ever has." That was Margaret Mead's conclusion after a lifetime of observing very diverse cultures around the world. Her insight has been borne out time and again throughout the development of this country of ours. Being allowed to live life in an atmosphere of religious freedom, having a voice in the government you support with your taxes, living free of lifelong enslavement by another person. These beliefs about how life should and must be lived were once considered outlandish by many. But these beliefs were fervently held by visionaries whose steadfast work brought about changed minds and attitudes. Now these beliefs are commonly shared across U.S. society.

Another initially outlandish idea that has come to pass: United States citizenship for women. 1998 marked the 150th Anniversary of a movement by women to achieve full civil rights in this country. Over the past seven generations, dramatic social and legal changes have been accomplished that are now so accepted that they go unnoticed by people whose lives they have utterly changed. Many people who have lived through the recent decades of this process have come to accept blithely what has transpired. And younger people, for the most part, can hardly believe life was ever otherwise. They take the changes completely in stride, as how life has always been.

The staggering changes for women that have come about over those seven generations in family life, in religion, in government, in employment, in education—these changes did not just happen spontaneously. Women themselves made these changes happen, very deliberately. Women have not been the passive recipients of miraculous changes in laws and human nature. Seven generations of women have come together to affect these changes in the most democratic ways:

Source: Eisenberg, Bonnie and Mary Ruthsdotter, "Living the Legacy: The Women's Rights Movement 1848–1998," *The National Women's History Project,* 1998. Reprinted with permission of Bonnie Eisenberg and Mary Ruthsdotter.

through meetings, petition drives, lobbying, public speaking, and nonviolent resistance. They have worked very deliberately to create a better world, and they have succeeded hugely.

Throughout 1998, the 150th anniversary of the Women's Rights Movement is being celebrated across the nation with programs and events taking every form imaginable. Like many amazing stories, the history of the Women's Rights Movement began with a small group of people questioning why human lives were being unfairly constricted.

A TEA LAUNCHES A REVOLUTION

The Women's Rights Movement marks July 13, 1848 as its beginning. On that sweltering summer day in upstate New York, a young housewife and mother, Elizabeth Cady Stanton, was invited to tea with four women friends. When the course of their conversation turned to the situation of women, Stanton poured out her discontent with the limitations placed on her own situation under America's new democracy. Hadn't the American Revolution been fought just 70 years earlier to win the patriots freedom from tyranny? But women had not gained freedom even though they'd taken equally tremendous risks through those dangerous years. Surely the new republic would benefit from having its women play more active roles throughout society. Stanton's friends agreed with her, passionately. This was definitely not the first small group of women to have such a conversation, but it was the first to plan and carry out a specific, large-scale program.

Today we are living the legacy of this afternoon conversation among women friends. Throughout 1998, events celebrating the 150th Anniversary of the Women's Rights Movement are looking at the massive changes these women set in motion when they daringly agreed to convene the world's first Women's Rights Convention.

Within two days of their afternoon tea together, this small group had picked a date for their convention, found a suitable location, and placed a small announcement in the Seneca County Courier. They called "A convention to discuss the social, civil, and religious condition and rights of woman." The gathering would take place at the Wesleyan Chapel in Seneca Falls on July 19 and 20, 1848.

In the history of western civilization, no similar public meeting had ever been called.

A "DECLARATION OF SENTIMENTS" IS DRAFTED

These were patriotic women, sharing the ideal of improving the new republic. They saw their mission as helping the republic keep its promise of better, more egalitarian lives for its citizens. As the women set about preparing for the event,

Elizabeth Cady Stanton used the Declaration of Independence as the framework for writing what she titled a "Declaration of Sentiments." In what proved to be a brilliant move, Stanton connected the nascent campaign for women's rights directly to that powerful American symbol of liberty. The same familiar words framed their arguments: "We hold these truths to be self-evident; that all men and women are created equal; that they are endowed by their Creator with certain inalienable rights; that among these are life, liberty, and the pursuit of happiness."

In this Declaration of Sentiments, Stanton carefully enumerated areas of life where women were treated unjustly. Eighteen was precisely the number of grievances America's revolutionary forefathers had listed in their Declaration of Independence from England.

Stanton's version read, "The history of mankind is a history of repeated injuries and usurpations on the part of man toward woman, having in direct object the establishment of an absolute tyranny over her. To prove this, let facts be submitted to a candid world." Then it went into specifics:

- Married women were legally dead in the eyes of the law
- Women were not allowed to vote
- Women had to submit to laws when they had no voice in their formation
- Married women had no property rights
- Husbands had legal power over and responsibility for their wives to the extent that they could imprison or beat them with impunity
- Divorce and child custody laws favored men, giving no rights to women
- Women had to pay property taxes although they had no representation in the levying of these taxes
- Most occupations were closed to women and when women did work they were paid only a fraction of what men earned
- Women were not allowed to enter professions such as medicine or law
- Women had no means to gain an education since no college or university would accept women students
- With only a few exceptions, women were not allowed to participate in the affairs of the church
- Women were robbed of their self-confidence and self-respect, and were made totally dependent on men

Strong words. . . . Large grievances. . . . And remember: This was just seventy years after the Revolutionary War. Doesn't it seem surprising to you that this unfair treatment of women was the norm in this new, very idealistic democracy? But this Declaration of Sentiments spelled out what was the status quo for European-American women in 1848 America, while it was even worse for enslaved Black women.

Elizabeth Cady Stanton's draft continued: "Now, in view of this entire disenfranchisement of one-half the people of this country, their social and religious degradation,—in view of the unjust laws above mentioned, and because women do feel themselves aggrieved, oppressed, and fraudulently deprived of their most sacred rights, we insist that they have immediate admission to all the rights and privileges which belong to them as citizens of these United States."

That summer, change was in the air and Elizabeth Cady Stanton was full of hope that the future could and would be brighter for women.

THE FIRST WOMEN'S RIGHTS CONVENTION

The convention was convened as planned, and over the two-days of discussion, the Declaration of Sentiments and 12 resolutions received unanimous endorsement, one by one, with a few amendments. The only resolution that did not pass unanimously was the call for women's enfranchisement. That women should be allowed to vote in elections was almost inconceivable to many. Lucretia Mott, Stanton's longtime friend, had been shocked when Stanton had first suggested such an idea. And at the convention, heated debate over the woman's vote filled the air.

Today, it's hard for us to imagine this, isn't it? Even the heartfelt pleas of Elizabeth Cady Stanton, a refined and educated woman of the time, did not move the assembly. Not until Frederick Douglass, the noted Black abolitionist and rich orator, started to speak, did the uproar subside. Woman, like the slave, he argued, had the right to liberty. "Suffrage," he asserted, "is the power to choose rulers and make laws, and the right by which all others are secured." In the end, the resolution won enough votes to carry, but by a bare majority.

The Declaration of Sentiments ended on a note of complete realism: "In entering upon the great work before us, we anticipate no small amount of misconception, misrepresentation, and ridicule; but we shall use every instrumentality within our power to effect our object. We shall employ agents, circulate tracts, petition the State and national Legislatures, and endeavor to enlist the pulpit and the press in our behalf. We hope this Convention will be followed by a series of Conventions, embracing every part of the country."

THE BACKLASH BEGINS

Stanton was certainly on the mark when she anticipated "misconception, misrepresentation, and ridicule." Newspaper editors were so scandalized by the shameless audacity of the Declaration of Sentiments, and particularly of the ninth resolution—women demanding the vote!—that they attacked the women with all the vitriol they could muster. The women's rights movement was only one day old and the backlash had already begun!

In ridicule, the entire text of the Declaration of Sentiments was often published, with the names of the signers frequently included. Just as ridicule today often has a squelching effect on new ideas, this attack in the press caused many people from the Convention to rethink their positions. Many of the women who had attended the convention were so embarrassed by the publicity that they actually withdrew their signatures from the Declaration. But most stood firm. And something the editors had not anticipated happened: Their negative articles about the women's call for expanded rights were so livid and widespread that they actually had a positive impact far beyond anything the organizers could have hoped for. People in cities and isolated towns alike were now alerted to the issues, and joined this heated discussion of women's rights in great numbers!

THE MOVEMENT EXPANDS

The Seneca Falls women had optimistically hoped for "a series of conventions embracing every part of the country." And that's just what did happen. Women's Rights Conventions were held regularly from 1850 until the start of the Civil War. Some drew such large crowds that people actually had to be turned away for lack of sufficient meeting space!

The women's rights movement of the late 19th century went on to address the wide range of issues spelled out at the Seneca Falls Convention. Elizabeth Cady Stanton and women like Susan B. Anthony, Lucy Stone, and Sojourner Truth traveled the country lecturing and organizing for the next forty years. Eventually, winning the right to vote emerged as the central issue, since the vote would provide the means to achieve the other reforms. All told, the campaign for woman suffrage met such staunch opposition that it took 72 years for the women and their male supporters to be successful.

As you might imagine, any 72-year campaign includes thousands of political strategists, capable organizers, administrators, activists and lobbyists. The story of diligent women's rights activism is a litany of achievements against tremendous odds, of ingenious strategies and outrageous tactics used to outwit opponents and make the most of limited resources. It's a dramatic tale, filled with remarkable women facing down incredible obstacles to win that most basic American civil right—the vote.

Among these women are several activists whose names and accomplishments should become as familiar to Americans as those of Thomas Jefferson, Abraham Lincoln and Martin Luther King, Jr.

- Elizabeth Cady Stanton, of course. And Susan B. Anthony. Matilda Joslyn Gage. Lucy Stone. They were pioneer theoreticians of the 19th-century women's rights movement.
- Esther Morris, the first woman to hold a judicial position, who led the first successful state campaign for woman suffrage, in Wyoming in 1869. Abigail Scott Duniway, the leader of the successful fight in Oregon and Washington in the early 1900s.

- Ida B. Wells-Barnett and Mary Church Terrell, organizers of thousands of African-American women who worked for suffrage for all women.
- Harriot Stanton Blatch, daughter of Elizabeth Cady Stanton, and Alice Stone Blackwell, Lucy Stone's daughter, who carried on their mothers' legacy through the next generation.
- Anna Howard Shaw and Carrie Chapman Catt, leaders of the National American Woman Suffrage Association in the early years of the 20th century, who brought the campaign to its final success.
- Alice Paul, founder and leader of the National Woman's Party, considered the radical wing of the movement.
- Ruth Bader Ginsburg, now a Supreme Court Justice, learned the story of the Women's Rights Movement. Today she says, "I think about how much we owe to the women who went before us—legions of women, some known but many more unknown. I applaud the bravery and resilience of those who helped all of us—you and me—to be here today."

AFTER THE VOTE WAS WON

After the vote was finally won in 1920, the organized Women's Rights Movement continued on in several directions. While the majority of women who had marched, petitioned and lobbied for woman suffrage looked no further, a minority—like Alice Paul—understood that the quest for women's rights would be an ongoing struggle that was only advanced, not satisfied, by the vote.

In 1919, as the suffrage victory drew near, the National American Woman Suffrage Association reconfigured itself into the League of Women Voters to ensure that women would take their hard-won vote seriously and use it wisely.

In 1920, the Women's Bureau of the Department of Labor was established to gather information about the situation of women at work, and to advocate for changes it found were needed. Many suffragists became actively involved with lobbying for legislation to protect women workers from abuse and unsafe conditions.

In 1923, Alice Paul, the leader of the National Woman's Party, took the next obvious step. She drafted an Equal Rights Amendment for the United States Constitution. Such a federal law, it was argued, would ensure that "Men and women have equal rights throughout the United States." A constitutional amendment would apply uniformly, regardless of where a person lived.

The second wing of the post-suffrage movement was one that had not been explicitly anticipated in the Seneca Falls "Declaration of Sentiments." It was the birth control movement, initiated by a public health nurse, Margaret Sanger, just as the suffrage drive was nearing its victory. The idea of woman's right to control her own body, and especially to control her own reproduction and sexuality, added a visionary new dimension to the ideas of women's emancipation. This movement not only endorsed educating women about existing birth control methods. It also spread the conviction that meaningful freedom for modern women meant they must be able to decide for themselves whether they would become mothers, and when. For decades, Margaret Sanger and her supporters faced down at every turn the zealously enforced laws denying women this right. In 1936, a Supreme Court decision declassified birth control information as obscene. Still, it was not until 1965 that married couples in all states could obtain contraceptives legally.

THE SECOND WAVE

So it's clear that, contrary to common misconception, the Women's Rights Movement did not begin in the 1960s. What occurred in the 1960s was actually a second wave of activism that washed into the public consciousness, fueled by several seemingly independent events of that turbulent decade. Each of these events brought a different segment of the population into the movement.

First: Esther Peterson was the director of the Women's Bureau of the Dept. of Labor in 1961. She considered it to be the government's responsibility to take an active role in addressing discrimination against women. With her encouragement, President Kennedy convened a Commission on the Status of Women, naming Eleanor Roosevelt as its chair. The report issued by that commission in 1963 documented discrimination against women in virtually every area of American life. State and local governments quickly followed suit and established their own commissions for women, to research conditions and recommend changes that could be initiated.

Then: In 1963, Betty Friedan published a landmark book, The Feminine Mystique. The Feminine Mystique evolved out of a survey she had conducted for her 20-year college reunion. In it she documented the emotional and intellectual oppression that middle-class educated women were experiencing because of limited life options. The book became an immediate bestseller, and inspired thousands of women to look for fulfillment beyond the role of homemaker.

Next: Title VII of the 1964 Civil Rights Act was passed, prohibiting employment discrimination on the basis of sex as well as race, religion, and national origin. The category "sex" was included as a last-ditch effort to kill the bill. But it passed, nevertheless. With its passage, the Equal Employment Opportunity Commission was established to investigate discrimination complaints. Within the commission's first five years, it received 50,000 sex discrimination complaints. But it was quickly obvious that the commission was not very interested in pursuing these complaints. Betty Friedan, the chairs of the various state Commissions on the Status of Women, and other feminists agreed to form a civil rights organization for women similar to the NAACP. In 1966, the National Organization for Women was organized, soon to be followed by an array of other mass-membership organizations addressing the needs of specific groups of women, including Blacks, Latinas, Asians-Americans, lesbians, welfare recipients, business owners, aspiring politicians, and tradeswomen and professional women of every sort.

During this same time, thousands of young women on college campuses were playing active roles within the anti-war and civil rights movement. At least, that was their intention. Many were finding their efforts blocked by men who felt leadership of these movements was their own province, and that women's roles should be limited to fixing food and running mimeograph machines. It wasn't long before these young women began forming their own "women's liberation" organizations to address their role and status within these progressive movements and within society at large.

NEW ISSUES COME TO THE FORE

These various elements of the re-emerging Women's Rights Movement worked together and separately on a wide range of issues. Small groups of women in hundreds of communities worked on grassroots projects like establishing women's newspapers, bookstores and cafes. They created battered women's shelters and rape crisis hotlines to care for victims of sexual abuse and domestic violence. They came together to form child care centers so women could work outside their homes for pay. Women health care professionals opened women's clinics to provide birth control and family planning counseling—and to offer abortion services—for low-income women. These clinics provided a safe place to discuss a wide range of health concerns and experiment with alternative forms of treatment.

With the inclusion of Title IX in the Education Codes of 1972, equal access to higher education and to professional schools became the law. The long-range effect of that one straightforward legal passage beginning "Equal access to education programs . . . ," has been simply phenomenal. The number of women doctors, lawyers, engineers, architects and other professionals has doubled and doubled again as quotas actually limiting women's enrollment in graduate schools were outlawed. Athletics has probably been the most hotly contested area of Title IX, and it's been one of the hottest areas of improvement, too. The rise in girls' and women's participation in athletics tells the story: One in twenty-seven high school girls played sports 25 years ago; one in three do today. The whole world saw how much American women athletes could achieve during the last few Olympic Games, measured in their astonishing numbers of gold, silver, and bronze medals. This was another very visible result of Title IX.

In society at large, the Women's Rights Movement has brought about measurable changes, too. In 1972, 26% of men and women said they would not vote for a woman for president. In 1996, that sentiment had plummeted to just over

5% for women and to 8% for men. The average age of women when they first marry has moved from twenty to twenty-four during that same period.

But perhaps the most dramatic impact of the women's rights movement of the past few decades has been women's financial liberation. Do you realize that just 25 years ago married women were not issued credit cards in their own name? That most women could not get a bank loan without a male co-signer? That women working full time earned fifty-nine cents to every dollar earned by men?

Help-wanted ads in newspapers were segregated into "Help wanted— women" and "Help wanted—men." Pages and pages of jobs were announced for which women could not even apply. The Equal Employment Opportunity Commission ruled this illegal in 1968, but since the EEOC had little enforcement power, most newspapers ignored the requirement for years. The National Organization for Women (NOW), had to argue the issue all the way to the Supreme Court to make it possible for a woman today to hold any job for which she is qualified. And so now we see women in literally thousands of occupations which would have been almost unthinkable just one generation ago: dentist, bus driver, veterinarian, airline pilot, and phone installer, just to name a few.

Many of these changes came about because of legislation and court cases pushed by women's organizations. But many of the advances women achieved in the 1960s and '70s were personal: getting husbands to help with the housework or regularly take responsibility for family meals; getting a long-deserved promotion at work; gaining the financial and emotional strength to leave an abusive partner.

THE EQUAL RIGHTS AMENDMENT IS RE-INTRODUCED

Then, in 1972, the Equal Rights Amendment, which had languished in Congress for almost fifty years, was finally passed and sent to the states for ratification. The wording of the ERA was simple: "Equality of rights under the law shall not be denied or abridged by the United States or by any state on account of sex." To many women's rights activists, its ratification by the required thirty-eight states seemed almost a shoo-in.

The campaign for state ratification of the Equal Rights Amendment provided the opportunity for millions of women across the nation to become actively involved in the Women's Rights Movement in their own communities. Unlike so many other issues which were battled-out in Congress or through the courts, this issue came to each state to decide individually. Women's organizations of every stripe organized their members to help raise money and generate public support for the ERA. Marches were staged in key states that brought out hundreds of thousands of supporters. House meetings, walk-a-thons, door-to-door canvassing, and events of every imaginable kind were held by ordinary women, many of whom had never done anything political in their lives before. Generous checks and single dollar bills poured into the campaign headquarters, and the ranks of NOW and other women's rights organizations swelled to historic sizes. Every women's magazine and most general interest publications had stories on the implications of the ERA, and the progress of the ratification campaign.

But Elizabeth Cady Stanton proved prophetic once again. Remember her prediction that the movement should "anticipate no small amount of misconception, misrepresentation, and ridicule"? Opponents of the Equal Rights Amendment, organized by Phyllis Schlafly, feared that a statement like the ERA in the Constitution would give the government too much control over our personal lives. They charged that passage of the ERA would lead to men abandoning their families, unisex toilets, gay marriages, and women being drafted. And the media, purportedly in the interest of balanced reporting, gave equal weight to these deceptive arguments just as they had when the possibility of women winning voting rights was being debated. And, just like had happened with woman suffrage, there were still very few women in state legislatures to vote their support, so male legislators once again had it in their power to decide if women should have equal rights. When the deadline for ratification came in 1982, the ERA was just three states short of the 38 needed to write it into the U.S. constitution. Seventy-five percent of the women legislators in those three pivotal states supported the ERA, but only 46% of the men voted to ratify.

Despite polls consistently showing a large majority of the population supporting the ERA, it was considered by many politicians to be just too controversial. Historically speaking, most if not all the issues of the women's rights movement have been highly controversial when they were first voiced. Allowing women to go to college? That would shrink their reproductive organs! Employ women in jobs for pay outside their homes? That would destroy families! Cast votes in national elections? Why should they bother themselves with such matters? Participate in sports? No lady would ever want to perspire! These and other issues that were once considered scandalous and unthinkable are now almost universally accepted in this country.

MORE COMPLEX ISSUES SURFACE

Significant progress has been made regarding the topics discussed at the Seneca Falls Convention in 1848. The people attending that landmark discussion would not even have imagined the issues of the Women's Rights Movement in the 1990s. Much of the discussion has moved beyond the issue of equal rights and into territory that is controversial, even among feminists. To name a few:

- Women's reproductive rights. Whether or not women can terminate pregnancies is still controversial twenty-five years after the Supreme Court ruling in Roe v. Wade affirmed women's choice during the first two trimesters.

- Women's enrollment in military academies and service in active combat. Are these desirable?
- Women in leadership roles in religious worship. Controversial for some, natural for others.
- Affirmative action. Is help in making up for past discrimination appropriate? Do qualified women now face a level playing field?
- The mommy track. Should businesses accommodate women's family responsibilities, or should women compete evenly for advancement with men, most of whom still assume fewer family obligations?
- Pornography. Is it degrading, even dangerous, to women, or is it simply a free speech issue?
- Sexual harassment. Just where does flirting leave off and harassment begin?
- Surrogate motherhood. Is it simply the free right of a woman to hire out her womb for this service?
- Social Security benefits allocated equally for homemakers and their working spouses, to keep surviving wives from poverty as widows.

Today, young women proudly calling themselves "the third wave" are confronting these and other thorny issues. While many women may still be hesitant to call themselves "feminist" because of the ever-present backlash, few would give up the legacy of personal freedoms and expanded opportunities women have won over the last 150 years. Whatever choices we make for our own lives, most of us envision a world for our daughters, nieces and granddaughters where all girls and women will have the opportunity to develop their unique skills and talents and pursue their dreams.

1998: LIVING THE LEGACY

In the 150 years since that first, landmark Women's Rights Convention, women have made clear progress in the areas addressed by Elizabeth Cady Stanton in her revolutionary Declaration of Sentiments. Not only have women won the right to vote; we are being elected to public office at all levels of government. Jeannette Rankin was the first woman elected to Congress, in 1916. By 1971, three generations later, women were still less than three percent of our congressional representatives. Today women hold only 11% of the seats in Congress, and 21% of the state legislative seats. Yet, in the face of such small numbers, women have successfully changed thousands of local, state, and federal laws that had limited women's legal status and social roles.

In the world of work, large numbers of women have entered the professions, the trades, and businesses of every kind. We have opened the ranks of the clergy, the military, the newsroom. More than three million women now work in occupations considered "nontraditional" until very recently.

We've accomplished so much, yet a lot still remains to be done. Substantial barriers to the full equality of America's women still remain before our freedom as a Nation can be called complete. But the Women's Rights Movement has clearly been successful in irrevocably changing the circumstances and hopes of women. The remaining injustices are being tackled daily in the courts and conference rooms, the homes and organizations, workplaces and playing fields of America.

Women and girls today are living the legacy of women's rights that seven generations of women before us have given their best to achieve. Alice Paul, that intrepid organizer who first wrote out the Equal Rights Amendment in 1923, said, "I always feel the movement is sort of a mosaic. Each of us puts in one little stone, and then you get a great mosaic at the end." Women, acting together, adding their small stones to the grand mosaic, have increased their rights against all odds, nonviolently, from an initial position of powerlessness. We have a lot to be proud of in this heroic legacy, and a great deal to celebrate on the occasion of the 150th Anniversary of the founding of the Women's Rights Movement.

Gay Rights

The gay rights movement comprises a collection of loosely aligned civil rights groups, human rights groups, support groups and political activists seeking acceptance, tolerance and equality for lesbian, gay, bisexual, and transgender people, and related causes. . . .

Although it is difficult to generalize, given the wide range of opinions and beliefs within the gay rights movement, in general most members agree upon the following points:

- in tolerance to all people regardless of their sexual orientation, gender identity or gender expression;
- that all people deserve equal rights and parity in law regardless of their sexual orientation, gender identity or gender expression;
- that homophobia (the irrational fear and/or hatred of homosexuals) as well as transphobia is dangerous, not just to gays and lesbians or transgender people, but to all members of society;
- views that consider homosexuality or gender variance to be negative (i.e. a sin or a perversion) are irrelevant, misguided or even outright malicious;
- that sexual orientation is innate and cannot be consciously changed, referring to homosexuality, heterosexuality and bisexuality equally as unchangeable sexual orientations;
- that gender identity is not a choice;
- that attempts to alter sexual orientation (see ex-gay, reparative therapy and gender identity) can be dangerous, misguided at best;
- that people should be free to express their sexual or gender identity without fear of reprisal and
- that homosexuality does not break down the fibers of the "traditional" family; homophobia does.

In the United States, the first gay rights movement was the Chicago *Society for Human Rights* in 1924. The movement was influenced by the German gay rights movement, and was shut down by the local police within a few months. After the Second World War there were initial steps toward a gay rights movement with

Source: http://en.wikipedia.org/wiki/Gay_Rights. Last modified 24 November 2005.

the formation of the Mattachine Society, the Daughters of Bilitis and ONE, Inc. and the publications of Phil Andros in the years immediately following World War II. Also during this time frame Sexual Behavior in the Human Male was published by Alfred Kinsey, a work which was one of the first to look scientifically at the subject of sexuality. Kinsey's incredible assertion, backed by a great deal of research, that approximately 10% of the male population (and about half that number among females) had, or would have, at least one overt homosexual experience during the course of their lifetime, was a dramatic departure from the prevailing beliefs of the time. Before its publication, homosexuality was not a topic of discussion, generally, but afterwards it began to appear even in mainstream publications such as *Time Magazine, Life Magazine*, and others.

Despite the entry of the subject into mainstream consciousness very little actual change in the laws or mores of society was seen until the mid-1960s, the time the "Sexual Revolution" began. This was a time of major social upheaval in many social areas, including views of sexuality. [In this context, gay people saw themselves as a minority group. They also became less and less willing to accept their status as social outcasts, sinners, and sick.] On June 27, 1969, a routine police raid on a gay bar (The Stonewall Inn) in Greenwich Village in New York City, sparked a riot that lasted over the weekend as gay men and lesbians converged to protest the police. These Stonewall riots were a turning point for the modern gay rights movement, as it was one of the first times in history in which a significant number of homosexual people resisted, thus ushering in a new wave of gay militancy (paraphrased from Geoffrey W. Bateman. "Gay Liberation Front," *GLBT: An Encyclopedia of Gay, Lesbian. Bisexual. Transgender. and Queer Culture.* www.glbtq.com/social-sciences/gay_liberation_front.html).]

The aftermath of the Stonewall riots saw the creation of such groups as the Gay Liberation Front (GLF) and the Gay Activists' Alliance (GAA) in New York City. The GLF's "A Gay Manifesto" set out the aims for the fledgling gay liberation movement, and influential intellectual Paul Goodman published his *The Politics of Being Queer* (1969). Chapters of the GLF then spread to other countries. These groups would be the seeds for the various modern gay rights groups that campaign for equality in countries around the globe. In the 1970s many gay people moved to San Francisco, where they rapidly acquired considerable political influence, including getting one of their number, Harvey Milk, elected to the city's Board of Supervisors, a legislative chamber often known as a City Council in other municipalities. Milk was assassinated in 1978 along with the city's mayor, George Moscone.

The first national gay rights march in the United States took place on October 14, 1979 in Washington, DC, involving perhaps as many 100,000 people.

In the 21st century, defending homosexuals against anti-gay bias and gay-bashing and other forms of discrimination is a major element of American gay rights, often portrayed as intrinsic to human rights. Indeed, one of the most influential gay rights groups in the U.S. is called the Human Rights Campaign.

The gay rights movement is often divided on ideological lines. Progressive gay rights organizations include the National Gay and Lesbian Task Force (NGLTF), Parents and Friends of Lesbians and Gays (PFLAG) and the Gay and Lesbian Alliance Against Defamation (GLAAD) and various local gay community centers. Conservative gay rights organizations include the Log Cabin Republicans, the Independent Gay Forum and even some libertarian gay rights organizations have arisen such as *Gays and Lesbians, or Individual Liberty* and the *Outfront Libertarians.*

The movement has been successful in some areas. By the end of the 20th Century sodomy laws were repealed or overturned in most American states, and those that still remained were ruled unconstitutional in the June 2003 ruling in *Lawrence v. Texas.* Many companies and local governments have clauses in their nondiscrimination policies that prohibit discrimination on the basis of sexual orientation. In some jurisdictions in the U.S., gay bashing is considered a hate crime and given a harsher penalty.

The U.S. state of Massachusetts allows same-sex marriage, and the states of Vermont and Connecticut provide civil union as an alternative to marriage. However, in many states, laws and constitutional amendments have been passed forbidding any recognition of same-sex marriage. Virginia law, the most far-reaching, forbids recognition of any benefits similar to those of marriage between people of the same sex.

Gay people are now permitted to adopt in some locations, although there are fewer locations where they may adopt children jointly with their partners. Other states have moved to ban gay adoption and foster care.

In the cultural arena, similar changes have taken place. Positive and realistic gay characters appear in some television programs and movies, although stereotypes and negative depictions are still visible.

The main opponents of the advances of the gay rights movement in the US have, in general, been the Christian right and other social conservatives, often under the aegis of the Republican Party. The Roman Catholic Church, or at least its hierarchy, has also been prominent among the movement's adversaries as opponents of gay marriage and same-sex acts. In the Roman Catholic Church, gay people themselves are not condemned, and are encouraged to live in celibacy, while the Church does condemn gay relationships and the sexual actions performed by gays. Regionally, opposition to the gay rights movement has been strongest in the Southern states.

The United States has no federal law protecting against discrimination in employment by private sector employers based on sexual orientation. However, 16 states, the District of Columbia, and over 140 cities and counties have enacted such bans. As of November 2005, the states banning sexual orientation discrimination in private sector employment are California, Connecticut, Hawaii, Illinois, Maine, Maryland, Massachusetts, Minnesota, Nevada, New Hampshire, New Jersey, New

Mexico, New York, Rhode Island, Vermont and Wisconsin.[1] (http://www.hre.org/worknet/nd/states_ban_dso.asp). Many of these laws also ban discrimination in other contexts, such as housing or public accommodation. A proposed bill to ban anti-gay employment discrimination nationwide, known as the Employment Nondiscrimination Act (ENDA), has been introduced in the U.S. Congress, but its prospects of passage are not believed to be good in the current Republican-controlled Congress.

On March 4, 1998, the Supreme Court of the United States ruled in the case *Oncale v. Sundowner Offshore Services* that federal laws banning on-the-job sexual harassment also applied when both parties are the same sex. The lower courts, however, have reached differing conclusions about whether this ruling applies to harassment motivated by antigay animus.

On November 7, 2003 the New Hampshire Supreme Court ruled in Blanchflower v. Blanchflower that sex between people of the same gender, one of whom is married, does not constitute adultery under New Hampshire law.

The Living Wage Movement

In 1994, an effective alliance between labor (led by AFSCME) and religious leaders (BUILD) in Baltimore launched a successful campaign for a local law requiring city service contractors to pay a living wage. Since then, strong community, labor, and religious coalitions have fought for and won similar ordinances in cities such as St. Louis, Boston, Los Angeles, Tucson, San Jose, Portland, Milwaukee, Detroit, Minneapolis, and Oakland—bringing the national living wage total to 122 ordinances. Today, more than 75 living wage campaigns are underway in cities, counties, states, and college campuses across the country. Taken collectively, these impressive instances of local grassroots organizing is now rightfully dubbed the national living wage movement, which syndicated columnist Robert Kuttner has described as "the most interesting (and underreported) grassroots enterprise to emerge since the civil rights movement . . . signaling a resurgence of local activism around pocketbook issues."

In short, living wage campaigns seek to pass local ordinances requiring private businesses that benefit from public money to pay their workers a living wage. Commonly, the ordinances cover employers who hold large city or county service contracts or receive substantial financial assistance from the city in the form of grants, loans, bond financing, tax abatements, or other economic development subsidies.

The concept behind any living wage campaign is simple: Our limited public dollars should not be subsidizing poverty-wage work. When subsidized employers are allowed to pay their workers less than a living wage, tax payers end up footing a double bill: the initial subsidy and then the food stamps, emergency medical, housing and other social services low wage workers may require to support themselves and their families even minimally. Public dollars should be leveraged for the public good—reserved for those private sector employers who demonstrate a commitment to providing decent, family-supporting jobs in our local communities.

Many campaigns have defined the living wage as equivalent to the poverty line for a family of four (currently $9.06 an hour), though ordinances that have

Source: "Living Wage Movement" from The Living Wage Resource Center online website, www.livingwagecampaign.org. Reprinted with permission of Acorn Living Wage Resource Center.

passed range from $6.25 to $13.00 an hour, with some newer campaigns pushing for even higher wages.

Increasingly, living wage coalitions are proposing other community standards in addition to a wage requirement, such as health benefits, vacation days, community hiring goals, public disclosure, community advisory boards, environmental standards, and language that supports union organizing.

Although each campaign is different, most share some common elements. Often spearheaded by ACORN, other community groups, union locals, or central labor councils, living wage campaigns are characterized by uniquely broad coalitions of local community, union, and religious leaders who come together to develop living wage principles, organize endorsements, draft ordinance language, and plan campaign strategy. The campaigns usually call for some degree of research into work and poverty in the area, research on city contracts, subsidies and related wage data, and often cost of living studies.

In addition, the strength of living wage efforts often lies in their ability to promote public education through flyering, petitioning, rallies, demonstrations targeting low wage employers, low-wage worker speak-outs, reports, and press conferences. Because most current living wage campaigns seek to pass legislative measures, campaigns also include lobbying and negotiations with elected officials such as city and county councilors, the mayor's office, and city staff.

Living Wage campaigns also provide opportunities for organizations that work to build a mass base of low income or working people to join-up, organize, and mobilize new members. Community organizers and labor unions can look to build membership during the campaign with neighborhood door-knocking, worksite organizing, house visits, neighborhood and workplace meetings, petition signature gathering, etc. and after the campaign on workplace and neighborhood living wage trainings, implementation fights with city agencies, and through campaigns targeting specific companies to meet or exceed living wage requirements.

So, what makes a collection of local policy decisions merit the title of a national "movement"? In short, both the economic context that gives rise to these efforts and the nature of the campaigns themselves make them important tools in the larger struggle for economic justice.

First, consider the economic realities facing low income people today: the failure of the minimum wage to keep pace with inflation (it now buys less than it did in the 1960's); the growing income gap between the rich and the poor; massive cuts in welfare and downward pressure on wages resulting from former recipients being forced into the labor market with no promise of jobs; the growth of service sector jobs where low wages are concentrated; the weakening of labor unions; rampant no-strings-attached corporate welfare that depletes tax dollars while keeping workers poor. The list goes on. Living Wage campaigns have arisen in response to all these pressures.

Given this context, living wage campaigns have the potential to have benefits that go beyond the immediate benefits to affected low wage workers and their families. Wherever they arise, living wage campaigns have the potential to:

- Build and sustain permanent and powerful community, labor, and religious coalitions that promote greater understanding and support of each other's work and create the potential to influence other important public policy debates
- Provide organizing opportunities that strengthen the institutions that represent and build power for low and moderate income people: community groups, labor unions, religious congregations
- Serve as a tool of political accountability, forcing our elected officials to take a stand on working people's issues, as well as engaging low and moderate income people in the political process
- Build leadership skills among low-income members of community organizations, unions, and congregations
- Raise the whole range of economic justice issues that gave rise to the living wage movement and affect the ability of low income families to live and work with dignity and respect

Despite the concerted efforts of business interests who consistently oppose these campaigns, "living wage" has become a household word and an exciting model of a successful local grassroots strategy. With new campaigns springing up every month, this movement shows no signs of slowing down.

_____ ADDITIONAL READINGS _____

Albelda, Randy, and Ann Withorn (eds.). 2002. *Lost Ground: Welfare Reform, Poverty, and Beyond.* Cambridge, MA: South End Press.

This anthology includes essays on poor and working-class activism.

Branch, Taylor. 1989. *Parting of the Waters*: *America in the King Years, 1954–63.* New York: Simon and Schuster Touchstone; 1999. *Pillar of Fire: America in the King Years, 1963–65.* New York: Simon and Schuster; 2006. *At Canaan's Edge, America in the King Years, 1965–68.* New York: Simon and Schuster.

This award-winning trilogy focuses on Martin Luther King, Jr.'s contributions to the civil rights movement.

Duberman, Martin. 1993. *Stonewall.* New York: Dutton.

This book is about the Stonewall riots and their impact on the gay rights movement.

The Nation. 2000. "The Century Just Past," (January 10/17).

This issue of *The Nation* provides the 100 most significant events of the twentieth century through the lens of its progressive politics. Thus, the events highlighted emphasize social justice, especially equal rights for people of color.

Russell, Marta. 1998. *Beyond Ramps: Disability at the End of the Social Contract.* Monroe, ME: Common Courage Press.

Ms. Russell is an articulate spokesperson for the disability rights movement.

CHAPTER 3

Social Movements Promoting Democracy

The writers of the U.S. Constitution devised a framework for a democratic political system hailed as being of, by, and for the people. The original Constitution, however, was not as democratic as is commonly believed. The founders were people of wealth and property. Excluded from the Constitutional Convention were slaves, indentured servants, women, and men who did not own property, so the Constitution did not reflect the interests of those groups (Zinn, 1980:90). The original Constitution as devised in 1787:

> did not provide for popular elections, except for the House of Representatives, where the qualifications were set by the state legislatures (which required property-holding for voting in almost all the states), and excluded women, Indians, slaves. The Constitution provided for Senators to be elected by the state legislators, for the President to be elected by electors chosen by the state legislators, and for the Supreme Court to be appointed by the President. (Zinn, 1980:95)

Because some provisions in the Constitution were undemocratic, the ensuing years, decades, and centuries witnessed numerous social movements aimed at greater inclusion. The selections in this chapter provide examples.

The first article focuses on an early example from the 1830s known as the Dorr Rebellion. Thomas Wilson Dorr was a member of the Rhode Island Assembly and took up the cause of changing the state constitution so that all white males could vote. At the time, only white men with property and their eldest sons could vote, which meant that only 40 percent of Rhode Island's white men were eligible. Dorr started a "suffrage party," and called a convention to frame a new state constitution. The resulting charter clashed with the one adopted by a rival party. As the selection describes, Dorr's rivals declared martial law. Hostilities ensued with Dorr's forces losing the battle. But they won the "war." In 1843 the Rhode Island General Assembly framed a new constitution liberalizing the right to vote to fit the objectives of the Dorr suffrage party movement.

In the second reading, Akhil Reed Amar chronicles "How Women Won the Vote." The women's suffrage movement began shortly after the Civil War in the late 1860s. It took sixty years to reach ratification of the Nineteenth Amendment.

Achieving the right to vote for women in America proved to be a long journey requiring great perseverence on the part of women who cared about their country and the meaning of its Constitution.

But for racial minorities the pathway was even longer, more jarring, and demanding. Blacks and other racial minorities were given the legal right to vote by the Fifteenth Amendment to the Constitution ratified in 1870. However, through various devices such as the all-white party primaries, poll taxes, literacy tests, and intimidation tactics commonly adopted in Southern states, most blacks were kept from voting for another ninety-five years. In 1964 the long drive toward suffrage for racial minorities culminated in "freedom summer." The third selection in this chapter describes the efforts by civil rights organizations with courageous black and white volunteers to challenge white power in Mississippi that summer. Despite encountering huge difficulties, including lynchings, they won. The Voting Rights Act, now the cornerstone of America's guarantee to include racial minorities in the democratic process, was passed by Congress in 1965.

The last two selections highlight the ongoing struggle toward democracy. Journalist Bill Moyers provides an overview of the progressive movement, which began in the late nineteenth century and continues today in an effort to contain the influence of money in politics. Finally, we provide the classic statement by the Students for a Democratic Society (SDS) that provides the rationale for the student revolution of the 1960s. It is an eloquent argument for participatory democracy that is just as relevant today as it was a half century ago.

REFERENCES_____

Zinn, Howard. 1980. *A People's History of the United States*. New York: Harper & Row.

Dorr Rebellion

PRECURSORS

Under Rhode Island's charter, originally received from King Charles II of England in 1663, only landowners could vote. At the time, when most of the citizens of the colonies were farmers, this was considered fairly democratic. By the 1840s landed property worth at least $134 was required in order to vote. However as the industrial revolution reached North America and people moved into the cities, it created large numbers of people who could not vote. By 1829, 60% of the state's free white males were ineligible to vote.

This was held by some to violate Article IV, Section 4 of the United States Constitution, which provides that "the United States shall guarantee to every state in this union a republican form of government." In short, many believed that an electorate made up of only 40% of the white males of the state (no one thought to mention women or any minorities) was un-republican and hence in violation of the Constitution.

Prior to the 1840s, several attempts were made to replace the colonial charter with a new state constitution that provided broader voting rights, but all failed. The Charter lacked a procedure for amendment. The legislature had consistently failed to liberalize the constitution by extending voting rights, enacting a bill of rights, or reapportioning the legislature. By 1840, Rhode Island was the only state without universal suffrage for white males.

THE REBELLION

In 1841, suffrage supporters, led by [Thomas Wilson] Dorr, gave up on attempts to change the system from within. In October, they held an extralegal **People's Convention** and drafted a new constitution that granted the vote to all white males with one year's residence. At the same time, the state legislature formed a rival convention and drafted the **Freemen's Constitution,** making some concessions to democratic demands.

The two constitutions were voted on late in the year, with the Freemen's Constitution being defeated in the legislature, largely by Dorr supporters, while the

Source: http.en.wikipedia.org/wiki/Dorr_Rebellion. Last modified 3 December 2005.

People's Convention version was overwhelmingly supported in a referendum in December. Although much of the support for the People's Convention constitution was from the newly-eligible voters, Dorr claimed that a majority of those eligible under the old constitution had also supported it, making it legal.

In early 1842, both groups organized elections of their own, leading to the elections of both Dorr and Samuel Ward King as Governor of Rhode Island in April. King showed no signs of introducing the new constitution, and when matters came to a head he declared martial law. On May 4, the state legislature requested the dispatch of United States troops to suppress the "lawless assemblages." President John Tyler decided to sit the issue out, replying that he believed that "the danger of domestic violence is hourly diminishing." Nevertheless Tyler, citing the U.S. Constitution, added that

> if resistance is made to the execution of the laws of Rhode Island, by such force as the civil peace shall be unable to overcome, it will be the duty of this Government to enforce the constitutional guarantee—a guarantee given and adopted mutually by all the original States.

Most of the state militiamen were newly enfranchised by the referendum and supported Dorr. The "Dorrites" led an unsuccessful attack against the Arsenal in Providence on May 19, 1842. Defenders of the Arsenal on the "Charterite" (those who supported the original charter) side included Dorr's father, Sullivan Dorr, and his uncle, Crawford Allen. At the time, these men owned the Bernon Mill Village in Woonsocket. After his defeat, Thomas Dorr and his supporters retreated to Chepachet where they hoped to reconvene the People's Convention.

Charterite forces were sent to Woonsocket to defend the village and to cut off the retreat of the Dorrite forces. The Charterites fortified a house in preparation for an attack, but it never came and the Dorr Rebellion simply fell apart shortly thereafter. Governor King issued a warrant for Dorr's arrest June 8 with a reward of $1000, increased June 29 to $5000. Dorr fled the state.

The Charterites, finally convinced of the strength of the suffrage cause, called another convention. In September 1842, a session of the Rhode Island General Assembly met at Newport, Rhode Island and framed a new state constitution, which was ratified by the old limited electorate, proclaimed by Governor King on January 23, 1843, and took effect in May. The new constitution greatly liberalized voting requirements by extending suffrage to any free white man who could pay a poll tax of $1, and was accepted by both parties.

DORR'S FATE

Dorr returned later in 1843, was found guilty of treason against the state, and sentenced in 1844 to solitary confinement and hard labor for life. The harshness of the sentence was widely condemned, and in 1845 Dorr, his health now broken, was released. He was restored to his civil rights in 1851, and in 1854 the court judgment against him was set aside.

How Women Won the Vote

AKHIL REED AMAR

In August 1920, with the ratification of the Nineteenth Amendment to the Constitution, some 10 million American women finally became the full political equals of men, eligible to vote in all local, state, and federal elections. In terms of sheer numbers, the Woman Suffrage Amendment represented the single biggest democratizing event in American history. Even the extraordinary feats of the Founding and Reconstruction had brought about the electoral empowerment or enfranchisement of people numbering in the hundreds of thousands, not millions.

Woman suffrage came as a thunderclap. As late as 1909, women voted on equal terms with men only in four western states, home to less than two percent of the nation's population. How did they get from the Wilderness to the Promised Land in so short a span? First, it's necessary to ask how they got from bondage to the Wilderness—that is, how they managed to get equal voting rights in four Rocky Mountain states in the late 19th century.

The process began when the Wyoming Territory broke new ground in 1869 and 1870 by giving women equal rights with men to vote in all elections and to hold office. Twenty years later, Wyoming entered the Union as the first woman-suffrage state. Colorado, Utah, and Idaho soon followed suit.

Conditions in the West were especially favorable for woman suffrage. Women were a rare and precious resource in the region; under the laws of supply and demand, men had to work that much harder to attract and keep them. The city of Cheyenne's leading newspaper was quick to tout the significance of woman suffrage: "We now expect at once quite an immigration of ladies to Wyoming. We say to them all, 'come on.' " Just as the Constitution's original promises of freedom and democracy in the 1780s were meant to entice skilled European immigrants to travel across the ocean, so these immigrants' pioneer grandsons evidently aimed to persuade American women to journey through the plains and over the mountains.

Source: "How Women Won the Vote" by Akhil Reed Amar, *Wilson Quarterly,* 29, Summer 2005, pp. 30–34. © 2005 by Akhil Reed Amar. All rights reserved c/o Writers Representatives LLC, New York, NY. Reprinted with permission.

The 1890 census provides some support for this admittedly crude theory. For every 100 native-born Wyoming males, there were only 58 native-born females. No other state had so pronounced a gender imbalance. Colorado and Idaho were the fifth and sixth most imbalanced states overall in 1890. The other early woman-suffrage state, Utah, had a somewhat higher percentage of women (a consequence of its early experience with polygamy), but even it had only 88 native-born females for every 100 native-born males, ranking it 11th among the 45 states in the mid-1890s. Also, the second, third, fourth, and seventh most imbalanced states—Montana, Washington, Nevada, and Oregon—would all embrace woman suffrage in the early 1910s, several years ahead of most other states. In all these places, men voting to extend the suffrage to women had little reason to fear that males might be outvoted en masse by females anytime soon.

The experience of other countries is also suggestive. In 1893, New Zealand became the first nation in the world to give women the vote in all elections— though it withheld from them the right to serve in Parliament until 1919. From one perspective, New Zealand's niche within the British Empire was not altogether different from Wyoming's within the United States: a remote outpost eager to attract new settlers, especially women. At the turn of the century, New Zealand males outnumbered females by a ratio of 9 to 8. Among certain communities of European immigrants, the gender imbalance exceeded 2 to 1.

Australia gave women the vote in national elections in 1902, when there were fewer than 90 non-indigenous females for every 100 non-indigenous males. Before and after Australia's continental enfranchisement, each of the six Australian states that united to form the nation in 1901 followed its own suffrage rules for elections to local parliaments. The least densely populated and most gender-imbalanced region, Western Australia, was the second-fastest to give women the vote. It did so in 1899, nearly a full decade before the most populous and gender-balanced area, Victoria, became the last Australian state to embrace woman suffrage.

In the United States, federal territorial policy also provided a modest if unintended spur to woman suffrage. In the 19th century, Congress tended to wait for a territory to achieve a certain critical population mass before admitting it to statehood, though no single formula applied in all places and at all times. Inhabitants of each western territory understood that rapid population growth would enhance prospects for early statehood, and each new woman brought not only herself but, in most cases, the possibility of future children.

In its early years, the story of woman suffrage was in some ways the converse of the black suffrage experience. Even as western men were talking about encouraging an influx of eastern women with the lure of suffrage, northern states between 1866 and 1868 were imposing black suffrage on the South while largely declining to embrace it for themselves—precisely because they wanted to discourage southern blacks from flooding north.

Later, the stories of black and woman suffrage converged. Indeed, the language of the Woman Suffrage Amendment repeated the wording of the Fifteenth Amendment verbatim, with "sex" simply substituted for "race" as an impermissible basis for disfranchisement: "The right of citizens of the United States to vote shall not be denied or abridged by the United States or by any State on account of sex."

Once large numbers of black men could vote in many states, the stage was set for universalization of the equal suffrage principle articulated in the Fifteenth Amendment. In the case of both blacks and women, white male lawmakers for whom the disfranchised had never voted proved more eager to grant them the vote than did the larger mass of voters.

As early as 1878, Elizabeth Cady Stanton and other women leaders began appearing before the U.S. Senate in support of a constitutional amendment that would do for women what the Fifteenth Amendment had done for blacks. Introduced by Senator A. A. Sargent of California, the proposed amendment had been drafted by the crusading suffragist Susan B. Anthony, in collaboration with Stanton. In 1920, this amendment would prevail in the exact form in which Anthony had initially drafted it—but only after Anthony's acolytes had transformed the landscape of state practice.

Between 1896 (when Utah and Idaho became the third and fourth woman-suffrage states) and 1909, no new states gave women the vote in general state or federal elections. Yet even in this period of seeming quiescence, powerful subterranean forces were at work. A few additional states joined an already substantial list of those willing to let women vote in school board elections or on other municipal matters. More important, merely by voting routinely in the Rocky Mountain West, women pioneers were proving by example that equal suffrage was an eminently sensible and thoroughly American practice suitable for adoption in other states.

Eventually, suffragists—inspired by early crusaders such as Anthony, Stanton, and Lucy Stone, and by the quieter examples of thousands of ordinary Rocky Mountain women—succeeded in spreading woman suffrage to neighboring western states. From this broad and expanding base the movement began to successfully colonize the East. In effect, western egalitarians aimed to even up the continental balance of trade: The East had sent bodies out west, but the idea of woman suffrage would migrate in the other direction, reprising the American Revolution itself, in which colonial children had sought to teach Mother England the true meaning of liberty.

The special challenge confronting suffragists was that in each and every non-suffrage state, voteless women somehow had to persuade male voters and male lawmakers to do the right thing and share the vote. Their ultimate success showed that men were not utterly indifferent to the voices of women. However, 56 full-blown state referendum campaigns and countless lobbying efforts before state legislatures, Congress, and national party conventions were needed to make the Anthony Amendment a reality.

From 1910 through 1914, the pace of reform quickened dramatically, as seven additional states—six in the West and Kansas in the Midwest—gave women full suffrage rights. Meanwhile, other democratic reforms were percolating to the top of the political agenda and capturing the national imagination. At the state level, provisions empowering voters to participate in initiatives, referendums, recalls, and direct primaries swept the country. At the federal level, the Seventeenth Amendment, providing for the direct election of senators, became law in 1913, less than a year after Congress proposed it. Corruption was out, and good government was in—and women were widely associated with the latter. The progressive politics of the era also placed strong emphasis on education and literacy, and in many places the literacy rates of women outstripped those of men.

Soon, various midwestern and eastern state legislatures began allowing women to vote for president, if not for members of Congress or state legislators. By the end of 1919, a dozen states fell into the presidential-suffrage-only category, and two more allowed women to vote generally in primary elections, including presidential primaries. These legal changes typically did not require amendment of a state constitution or a direct appeal to the voters. Presidential suffrage thus offered a handy hedge for many a state lawmaker who hesitated to get too far ahead of his (currently all-male) voting base but who also saw that one day—soon—women would be voting even in state races.

Meanwhile, more states—including, for the first time, eastern and midwestern heavy-weights such as New York (in 1917) and Michigan (in 1918)—were clambering aboard the full-suffrage bandwagon. By the end of 1918, women had won full suffrage rights in a grand total of 15 of the 48 states then in the Union. Because federal lawmakers in all these places would now need to woo female as well as male voters, suffragists could look forward to strong support in Congress from this bloc. Eventually, members of Congress from full-suffrage states would favor the Nineteenth Amendment by a combined vote of 116 to 6, adding extra heft to the House support and providing the decisive margin of victory in the Senate.

True, in some places during the mid-1910s, woman suffrage went down to defeat. For example, in 1912 male voters in Ohio, Wisconsin, and Michigan said no, and in 1915 suffragists lost in Massachusetts, Pennsylvania, New Jersey, and New York. But by this point, savvy politicians were beginning to appreciate the mathematical logic of what historian Alexander Keyssar has aptly labeled the suffrage "endgame." Once women got the vote in a given state, there would be no going back. Unlike southern blacks, women would likely always have enough votes to keep the ballot after they first got it. Conversely, whenever suffragists failed to win the vote in a given state, they would be free to raise the issue again and again and again: Tomorrow would always be another day, and democracy's ratchet would inexorably do its work. Thus, New York women won in 1917 what they had failed to win in 1915, and suffragists prevailed in Michigan in 1918 after two earlier defeats.

Another aspect of the endgame: If and when women did get the vote, woe unto the diehard antisuffrage politician who had held out until the bitter end! Each state legislator or congressman from a nonsuffrage state had to heed not just the men who had elected him but also the men *and women* who could refuse to reelect him once the franchise was extended. (And with the ratification of the Seventeenth Amendment in 1913, which put an end to the selection of U.S. senators by state legislatures, senators also had to be responsive to this broader constituency.) The experience in Ohio, where male voters had refused to enfranchise women in 1912 and again in 1914, nicely illustrated the underlying electoral math. Senator Warren Harding voted for the Woman Suffrage Amendment and went on to capture the White House in 1920. Conversely, Senator Atlee Pomerene opposed the amendment and was voted out of office in 1922.

By the end of 1919, with 29 states already having adopted full or partial suffrage, no serious presidential candidate could afford to be strongly antisuffrage. To win the White House without several of these states would be the political equivalent of filling an inside straight. Even a senator from a nonsuffrage state had to think twice about opposing woman suffrage if he harbored any long-term presidential aspirations.

America's decision to enter World War I added still more momentum to the movement. In a military crusade being publicly justified as a war to "make the world safe for democracy," the claims of those Americans excluded from full democratic rights took on special urgency. Because America claimed to be fighting for certain ideals, it became especially important to live up to them. All across Europe, women were winning the vote in countries such as Norway, Denmark, Holland, Sweden, and even Austria and Germany. Surely, suffragists argued, the United States should not lag behind.

Also, women on the home front were making vital contributions to the general war effort, even if they did not bear arms on the battlefield. In a word, America's women were loyal—as America's blacks had been in the 1860s—and wars generally serve to remind nations of the value of loyalty. Given that a disproportionately high percentage of women across the country were American born, the nation's widespread nativist anxiety about German aliens in America, and even about naturalized citizens from Central Europe, also fueled the suffrage crusade.

Wars also generally increase executive power, and World War I was no exception. In September 1918, President Woodrow Wilson dramatized his support for the Woman Suffrage Amendment by appearing in person before the Senate to plead for constitutional reform. Reminding his audience that women were "partners . . . . in this war," Wilson proclaimed the amendment a "vitally necessary war measure" that would capture the imagination of "the women of the world" and enhance America's claim to global moral leadership in the post–war era. Several months after this flamboyant presidential intervention, Congress formally proposed the amendment. The endgame had entered its final stage.

The scene then shifted back to the states. In Congress, opponents of suffrage had unsuccessfully urged that the amendment be sent for ratification not to the 48 regular state legislatures but to ad hoc state conventions, as permitted by Article V of the Constitution. State ratifying conventions probably would have approximated referendums, because one-time convention delegates wouldn't have worried about their political futures. Supporters of the amendment resisted; they faced better odds with state legislatures.

In the final stage of the struggle for woman suffrage, the only major opposition to the Susan B. Anthony Amendment (as it was generally called) came from the South. White southerners, who by the turn of the century had effectively nullified the Black Suffrage Amendment in their region, had little sympathy for a Woman Suffrage Amendment written in parallel language and reaffirming the root principles of national voting rights and national enforcement power. In late August 1920, Tennessee put the Anthony Amendment over the top, becoming the 36th state to vote for ratification, but it was only the third of the 11 ex-Confederate states to say yes.

Read narrowly, the Nineteenth Amendment guaranteed women's equal right to vote in elections. Yet its letter and spirit swept even further, promising that women would bear equal rights and responsibilities in all political domains. In 1787, the amended Constitution consistently referred to the president with the words "he" and "his"—never "she" or "her." Yet today, no one doubts that women have an equal right to run for president. At the Founding, a jury meant, "twelve men, good and true." No longer. And once, every member of the federal legislature was a "congressman," and every Supreme Court member bore the title "Mr. Justice." No more—all thanks to an extraordinary amendment that literally changed the face of American government.

Mississippi and Freedom Summer

LISA COZZENS

"This is Mississippi, the middle of the iceberg."

—Bob Moses

In the early 1960s, Mississippi was the poorest state in the nation. 86% of all non-white families lived below the national poverty line.[1] In addition, the state had a terrible record of black voting rights violations. In the 1950s, Mississippi was 45% black, but only 5% of voting age blacks were registered to vote.[2] Some counties did not have a single registered black voter. Whites insisted that blacks did not want to vote, but this was not true. Many blacks wanted to vote, but they worried, and rightfully so, that they might lose their job. In 1962, over 260 blacks in Madison County overcame this fear and waited in line to register. 50 more came the next day. Only seven got in to take the test over the two days, walking past a sticker on the registrar's office door that bore a Confederate battle flag next to the message "Support Your Citizens' Council."[3] Once they got in, they had to take a test designed to prevent them from becoming registered. In 1954, in response to increasing literacy among blacks, the test, which originally asked applicants to "read *or* interpret" a section of the state constitution, was changed to ask applicants to "read *and* interpret" that document.[4] This allowed white registrars to decide whether or not a person passed the test. Most blacks, even those with doctoral degrees, "failed." In contrast, most whites passed, no matter what their education level. In George County, one white applicant's interpretation of the section "There shall be no imprisonment for debt" was "I thank that a Neorger should have 2 years in collage before voting because he don't under stand." (sic)[5] He passed.

    The NAACP went to Mississippi in an effort to register more blacks in the late 1950s. Amzie Moore, a local NAACP leader in Mississippi, met with SNCC worker Robert Parris Moses when Moses traveled through the state in July 1960, recruiting people for a SNCC conference. Moore encouraged

Source: "Mississippi & Freedom Summer" by Lisa Cozzens, from "The Civil Rights Movement, 1955–1965," *African American History,* June 29, 1988, on website www.watson.org. Reprinted by permission of the author.

Moses to bring more SNCC workers to the state, and the following summer he did, beginning a month-long voter registration campaign in the town of McComb, in conjunction with C. C. Bryant of the NAACP. SNCC organized a voter registration education program, teaching a weekly class that showed people how to register.

SNCC worker Marion Barry arrived on August 18 and started workshops to teach young blacks nonviolent protest methods. Many of the blacks, too young to vote, jumped at the opportunity to join the movement. They began holding sit-ins. Some were arrested and expelled from school. More were expelled when they held a protest march after the murder of Herbert Lee, who had helped SNCC workers, on September 25. In response to these expulsions, Moses and Chuck McDew started Nonviolent High School to teach the expelled students. They were arrested and sentenced to four months in jail for "contributing to the delinquency of minors."[6]

Other protests by blacks were met with violence. At sit-ins which began on May 28, 1963, participants were sprayed with paint and had pepper thrown in their eyes. Students who sang movement songs during lunch after the bombing of NAACP field director Medgar Evers' home were beaten. Evers himself was the most visible target for violence. He was a native of Mississippi and World War II veteran who was greeted by a mob of gun-wielding whites when he attempted to register after the war in his hometown of Decatur. He later said, "We fought during the war for America, Mississippi included. Now, after the Germans and Japanese hadn't killed us, it looked as though the white Mississippians would." After he was denied admission to the University of Mississippi law school, he went to work for the NAACP. By 1963, Evers was aware that, in the words of his wife Myrlie Evers,

> . . . Medgar was a target because he was the leader. The whole mood of white Mississippi was that if Medgar Evers were eliminated, the problem would be solved. . . . And we came to realize, in those last few days, last few months, that our time was short; it was simply in the air. You knew that something was going to happen, and the logical person for it to happen to was Medgar.

At an NAACP rally on June 7, Medgar Evers told the crowd, "Freedom has never been free . . . I love my children and I love my wife with all my heart. And I would die, and die gladly, if that would make a better life for them."[7] Five days later, he was shot and killed as he returned home around midnight. Byron de la Beckwith, a member of the Citizens' Council, was arrested for Evers' murder, but he was set free after two trials ended in hung juries. He later ran for lieutenant governor.

That fall, the Council of Federated Organizations (COFO), an umbrella organization of local and national civil rights groups founded in 1962, organized the Freedom Vote. The Freedom Vote had two main goals:

1. To show Mississippi whites and the nation that blacks wanted to vote and
2. To give blacks, many of whom had never voted, practice in casting a ballot

The mock vote pitted the actual candidates against candidates from the interracial Freedom Party. 60 white students from Yale and Stanford Universities came to Mississippi to help spread word of the Freedom Vote. 93,000 voted on the mock election day, and the Freedom Party candidates easily won.[8]

After the success of the Freedom Vote, SNCC decided to send volunteers into Mississippi during the summer of 1964, a presidential election year, for a voter registration drive. It became known as Freedom Summer. Bob Moses outlined the goals of Freedom Summer to prospective volunteers at Stanford University:

1. to expand black voter registration in the state
2. to organize a legally constituted "Freedom Democratic Party" that would challenge the whites-only Mississippi Democratic party
3. to establish "freedom schools" to teach reading and math to black children
4. to open community centers where indigent blacks could obtain legal and medical assistance[9]

800 students gathered for a week-long orientation session at Western College for Women in Oxford, Ohio, that June. They were mostly white and young, with an average age of 21. They were also from well-to-do families, as the volunteers had to bring $500 for bail as well as money for living expenses, medical bills, and transportation home. SNCC's James Forman told them to be prepared for death. "I may be killed. You may be killed. The whole staff may go." He also told them to go quietly to jail if arrested, because "Mississippi is not the place to start conducting constitutional law classes for the policemen, many of whom don't have a fifth-grade education."[10]

On June 21, the day after the first 200 recruits left for Mississippi from Ohio, three workers, including one volunteer, disappeared. Michael Schwerner, Andrew Goodman, and James Chaney had been taken to jail for speeding charges but were later released. What happened next is not known. Local police were called when the men failed to perform a required check-in with Freedom Summer headquarters, but Sheriff Lawrence Rainey was convinced the men were hiding to gain publicity. The FBI did not get involved for a full day. During the search for the missing workers, the FBI uncovered the bodies of three lynched blacks who had been missing for some time. The black community noted wryly that these murders received nowhere near the same nationwide media attention as the murders of the three workers, two of whom were white.

Meanwhile, Freedom Summer went on. Only a handful of recruits left the orientation session in Ohio. The volunteers helped provide basic services to blacks in the South. "Freedom clinics" provided health care; Northern lawyers worked in legal clinics to secure basic constitutional rights; "freedom schools," though illegal, taught blacks of all ages traditional subjects as well as black history.[11]

One of Freedom Summer's most important projects was the establishment of the Mississippi Freedom Democratic Party (MFDP) to challenge the all-white regular Democratic party in the state. This project actually started before Freedom Summer did, when MFDP won crucial support from the California Democratic Council, a liberal subsection of the state's Democratic party, and Joseph Rauh, head of the DC Democratic Party, vice president of Americans for Democratic Action (ADA), and general counsel to the United Auto Workers. President Johnson, however, backed the regular Democratic party because he could not afford to lose their political support.[12]

In June, the names of four MFDP candidates were on the Democratic primary ballot as delegates to be sent to the Democratic National Convention in Atlantic City, but all four lost. Later that month, the regular Democratic party adopted a platform that explicitly rejected the national party platform in the area of civil rights. This put President Johnson in a difficult position. The national Democratic organization required all delegates to make a pledge of party loyalty, but Johnson had to allow the Mississippi Democrats to be seated because otherwise delegates from five other states would walk out. The Mississippi issue was turning what should have been a quiet, routine convention into a racial battleground.

On August 4, the bodies of the three civil rights workers were found in a dam on a farm near Philadelphia, Mississippi. They had all been shot and the one black, James Chaney, had been brutally beaten. The discovery shifted media attention back to Mississippi just 18 days before the start of the Democratic National Convention. Two days later, the MFDP held a convention and selected a 68-person delegation, which included four whites, to go to the national convention. By now, the party had the support of ADA, delegates from nine states, and 25 congressmen. The delegates wanted to be seated instead of the regular delegates at the convention. To do so, they had to persuade eleven of the more than 100 members of the Credentials Committee to vote in their favor. They decided to provide testimony detailing how difficult it was for blacks to vote in Mississippi. Fannie Lou Hamer, one of twenty children of Mississippi sharecroppers, gave an impassioned speech to the Committee:

> If the Freedom Democratic Party is not seated now, I question America. Is this America? The land of the free and the home of the brave? Where we have to sleep with our telephones off the hook, because our lives be threatened daily?[13]

President Johnson quickly called a press conference to turn news cameras away from Atlantic City, but the evening news that night showed portions of Hamer's testimony. Her emotional statement moved people around the nation.

Senator Hubert Humphrey offered a compromise, with the blessing of the president. The white delegates would be seated if they pledged loyalty to the party platform. Two MFDP delegates, Aaron Henry and Ed King would also be seated, but as at-large delegates, not Mississippi delegates. Neither side liked the agreement, but in the end, both sides accepted. The trouble, however, was not over. When all but three of the Mississippi delegates refused to pledge allegiance to the party, the MFDP delegates borrowed passes from sympathetic delegates and took the seats vacated by the Mississippi delegates until they were thrown out. The next day, they returned. The empty seats had been removed, so the delegates just stood and sang freedom songs.

In the end, the Mississippi Freedom Democratic Party, like the Freedom Riders, did not fully accomplish its goals. The MFDP, however, was far from a failure. It showed blacks that they could have political power. It ensured that, in the words of Joe Rauh of ADA, "there will never be a lily-white [delegation] again."[14] It raised the important issue of voting rights, reminding America that the recently-passed Civil Rights Act, which disappointed black leaders because it did not address the right to vote, was not enough. It also helped blacks and other minorities gain more representation in the Democratic party. Freedom Summer, too, was an overall success. Clayborne Carson wrote:

> *When freedom school students from across the state gathered for a convention early in August, their increased confidence and political awareness were manifest in their approval of resolutions asking for enforcement of the Civil Rights Act of 1964, . . . elimination of the poll tax, and many other reforms.*[15]

There is no denying the effect that Freedom Summer had on Mississippi's blacks. In 1964, 6.7% of Mississippi's voting-age blacks were registered to vote, 16.3% below the national average. By 1969, that number had leaped to 66.5%, 5.5% above the national average.[16]

NOTES

1. Steven Kasher, *The Civil Rights Movement: A Photographic History, 1954–68* (New York: Abbeville Press, 1996):132–135.
2. Juan Williams, *Eyes on the Prize: America's Civil Rights Years, 1954–1965* (New York: Viking Penguin, 1987):208.
3. Anthony Lewis, *Portrait of a Decade: The Second American Revolution* (New York: Random House, 1964):135.
4. Williams, op. cit., p. 225.

5. Lewis, op. cit., p. 130.
6. Williams, op. cit., p. 213.
7. Ibid., pp. 208–222.
8. Ibid., p. 228.
9. Ibid., p. 229.
10. Ibid., p. 230.
11. Ibid., pp. 232–233.
12. Ibid., pp. 233–234.
13. Ibid., p. 241.
14. Ibid., p. 243.
15. Clayborne Carson, David J. Garrow, Gerald Gill, Vincent Harding, and Darlene Clark Hine (eds.), *The Eyes on the Prize Civil Rights Reader* (New York: Penguin Books, 1997):121.
16. Kasher, op. cit., pp. 172–173.

The Progressive Movement

BILL MOYERS

[W]e are heirs of a great movement, the Progressive movement, which began late in the nineteenth century and remade the American experience piece by piece until it peaked in the last third of the twentieth century. (I call it the Progressive movement for lack of a more precise term.) Its aim was to keep blood pumping through the veins of democracy when others were ready to call in the mortician. Progressives exalted and extended the original American Revolution. They spelled out new terms of partnership between the people and their rulers. And they kindled a flame that lit some of the most prosperous decades in modern history, not only here but in aspiring democracies everywhere, especially those of Western Europe.

Step back with me to the curtain-raiser, the founding convention of the People's Party—better known as the Populists—in 1892. Mainly cotton and wheat farmers from the recently reconstructed South and the newly settled Great Plains, they had come on hard, hard times, driven to the wall by falling prices for their crops on one hand and by racking interest rates, freight charges, and supply costs, on the other: all this in the midst of a booming and growing industrial America. They were angry, and their platform—issued deliberately on the Fourth of July—pulled no punches. "We meet," it said, "in the midst of a nation brought to the verge of moral, political and material ruin. . . . Corruption dominates the ballot box, the [state] legislatures and the Congress and touches even the bench. . . . The newspapers are largely subsidized or muzzled, public opinion silenced. . . . The fruits of the toil of millions are boldly stolen to build up colossal fortunes for a few."

Furious words indeed from rural men and women who were traditionally conservative and whose memories of taming the frontier were fresh and personal, but who in their fury invoked an American tradition as powerful as frontier individualism, namely, the war on inequality—especially government's role in promoting and preserving inequality by favoring the rich. The Founding Fathers turned their backs on the idea of property qualifications for holding office under the Constitution because they wanted absolutely no "veneration for wealth" in

Source: From *Moyers on America: A Journalist and His Times* by Bill Moyers, (New York: Random House, Anchor, 2004). Reprinted by permission.

the document. Thomas Jefferson, while claiming no interest in politics, built up a Democratic-Republican party to take the government back from the speculators and "stock-jobbers" who were in the saddle in 1800. Andrew Jackson slew the monster Second Bank of the United States, the six-hundred-pound gorilla of the credit system in the 1830s, in the name of the people versus the aristocrats who sat on the bank's governing board.

All these leaders were on record in favor of small government, but their opposition wasn't simply to government as such. They objected to government's power to confer *privilege* on the democracy's equivalent of the royal favorites of monarchist days: on the rich, on the insiders, on what today we know as the crony capitalists. The Populists knew it was the government that granted millions of acres of public land to the railroad builders. It was the government that gave the manufacturers of farm machinery a monopoly of the domestic market by a protective tariff that was no longer necessary to shelter infant industries. It was the government that contracted the national currency and sparked a deflationary cycle that crushed debtors and fattened the wallets of creditors. And those who made the great fortunes used them to buy the legislative and judicial favors that kept them on top. So the Populists recognized one great principle: the job of preserving equality of opportunity and democracy demanded the end of any unholy alliance between government and wealth. It was, to quote that platform again, "from the same womb of *governmental injustice*" that tramps and millionaires were bred (emphasis added).

The question remained, however: how was the democratic revolution to be revived, the promise of the Declaration reclaimed? How were Americans to restore government to its job of promoting the *general* welfare? And here the Populists made a break-through to another principle. In a modern, large-scale, industrial, and nationalized economy it wasn't enough simply to curb the government's outreach. Such a policy would simply leave power in the hands of the great corporations whose existence was inseparable from growth and progress. The answer was to turn government into an active player in the economy, at the very least enforcing fair play and when necessary being the friend, the helper, and the agent of the people at large in the contest against entrenched power. As a result, the Populist platform called for government loans to farmers about to lose their mortgaged homesteads, for government granaries to grade and store their crops fairly, for governmental inflation of the currency (a classical plea of debtors), and for some decidedly nonclassical actions: government ownership of the railroad, telephone, and telegraph systems; a graduated (i.e., progressive) tax on incomes; a flat ban on subsidies to "any private corporation." Moreover, in order to ensure that the government stayed on the side of the people, the party called for two electoral reforms, the initiative and referendum and the direct election of senators.

Predictably, the Populists were denounced, feared, and mocked as fanatical hayseeds ignorantly playing with socialist fire. They received twenty-two electoral votes for their 1892 candidate, plus some congressional seats and state houses, but this would prove to be the party's peak. America wasn't—and probably still isn't—ready for a new major party. The People's Party was a spent rocket by 1904. At the same time, when political organizations perish, their key ideas endure, and this is a perspective of great importance to today's progressives. Much of the Populist agenda would become law within a few years of the party's extinction because their goals were generally shared by a rising generation of young Republicans and Democrats who, justly or not, were seen as less outrageously outdated than the embattled farmers. These were the Progressives, the intellectual forebears of those of us who today call ourselves by the same name.

They were a diverse lot, held together by a common admiration of progress—hence the name—and a shared dismay at the paradox of poverty stubbornly persisting in the midst of progress like an unwanted guest at a wedding. Of course they welcomed, just as we do, the new marvels in the gift bag of technology—the telephones, the automobiles, the electrically powered urban transport and lighting systems, the indoor heating and plumbing, the processed foods and home appliances and machine-made clothing that reduced the sweat and drudgery of homemaking and were affordable to an ever-swelling number of people. At the same time, however, they saw the underside: the slums lurking in the shadows of the glittering cities; the exploited and unprotected workers whose low-paid labor filled the horn of plenty for others; the misery of those whom age, sickness, accident, or hard times condemned to servitude and poverty with no hope of comfort or security.

Incredibly, in little more than a century, the still-young revolution of 1776 was being strangled by the hard grip of a merciless ruling class. The large corporations that were called into being by modern industrialism after 1865—the end of the Civil War—had combined into trusts capable of making minions of both politics and government. What Henry George called "an immense wedge" was being forced through American society by "the maldistribution of wealth, status, and opportunity." . . .

[W]hat troubled our Progressive forebears was not only the miasma of poverty in their nostrils but also the sour stink of a political system for sale. The United States Senate was a millionaires' club. Money given to the political machines that controlled nominations could buy controlling influence in city halls, statehouses, and even courtrooms. Reforms and improvements ran into the immovable resistance of the almighty dollar. What, Progressives wondered, what would this do to the principles of popular government? All of them, whatever their political party, were inspired by the gospel of democracy. Inevitably, this swept them into the currents of politics, whether as active officeholders or persistent advocates. . . .

To be sure, these Progressives weren't saintly. Their glory years coincided with the heyday of lynching and segregation, of empire and the Big Stick and the bold theft of the Panama Canal, of immigration restriction and ethnic stereotypes.

Some were themselves businessmen only hoping to control an unruly market-place by regulation. By and large, however, they were conservative reformers. They aimed to preserve the existing balance between wealth and commonwealth. Their common enemy was unchecked privilege, their common hope was a better democracy, and their common weapon was informed public opinion.

In a few short years the Progressive spirit made possible the election not only of reform mayors and governors but of national figures such as Senator George Norris of Nebraska, Senator Robert M. La Follette of Wisconsin, and even that hard-to-classify political genius, Theodore Roosevelt, all three of them Republicans.

Here is the simplest laundry list of what was accomplished at the state and federal levels: publicly regulated or owned transportation, sanitation, and utilities system; the partial restoration of competition in the marketplace through improved antitrust laws; increased fairness in taxation; expansion of the public education and juvenile justice systems; safer workplaces and guarantees of compensation to workers injured on the job; oversight of the purity of water, medicines, and foods; conservation of the national wilderness heritage against overdevelopment; honest bidding on any public mining, lumbering, and ranching. All those safeguards were provided not by the automatic workings of free enterprise but by implementing the idea in the Declaration of Independence that the people had a right to governments that best promoted their "safety and happiness."

The mighty Progressive wave peaked in 1912, but the ideas unleashed by it forged the politics of the twentieth century. Like his cousin Theodore, Franklin Roosevelt argued that the real enemies of enlightened capitalism were "the male-factors of great wealth"—the "economic royalists"—from whom capitalism would have to be saved by reform and regulation. Progressive government became an embedded tradition of Democrats—the heart of Franklin Roosevelt's New Deal and Harry Truman's Fair Deal. Even Dwight D. Eisenhower honored this tradition; he did not want to tear down the house Progressives' ideas had built, only put it under different managers. The Progressive impulse had its final fling in the landslide of 1964, when Lyndon Johnson—a son of the west Texas hill country, where the Populist rebellion had been nurtured in the 1890s—won the public endorsement for what he meant to be the capstone in the arch of the New Deal.

I had a modest role in that era. I shared in its exhilaration and its failures. We went too far too fast, overreached at home and in Vietnam, failed to examine some assumptions, and misjudged the rising discontents and fierce backlash engendered by the passions of the time. Democrats grew so proprietary in Washington, D.C., that a corpulent, complacent political establishment couldn't recognize its own intellectual bankruptcy or see the Beltway encircling it and beginning to separate it from the working people of America. The failure of Democratic politicians and public thinkers to respond to popular discontents—to the daily lives of workers, consumers, parents, and ordinary taxpayers—allowed a resurgent conservatism to convert public concern and hostility into a crusade that masked the resurrection of social Darwinism as a moral philosophy, multinational corporations as a governing class, and the theology of markets as a transcendental belief system. . . .

What will it take to get back in the fight? The first order of business is to understand the real interests and deep opinions of the American people. What are these?

- That a Social Security card is not a private portfolio statement but a membership ticket in a society where we all contribute to a common treasury so that none need face the indignities of poverty in old age
- That tax evasion is not a form of conserving investment capital but a brazen abandonment of responsibility to the country
- That income inequality is not a sign of freedom of opportunity at work, because if it persists and grows, then unless you believe that some people are naturally born to ride and some to wear saddles, it's a sign that opportunity is less than equal
- That self-interest is a great motivator for production and progress but is amoral unless contained within the framework of social justice
- That the rich have the right to buy more cars than anyone else, more homes, vacations, gadgets, and gizmos, but they do not have the right to buy more democracy than anyone else
- That public services, when privatized, serve only those who can afford them and weaken the sense that we all rise and fall together as "one nation, indivisible"
- That concentration in the production of goods may sometimes be useful and efficient, but monopoly over the dissemination of ideas is tyranny
- That prosperity requires good wages and benefits for workers
- That our nation can no more survive as half democracy and half oligarchy than it could survive half slave and half free, and that keeping it from becoming all oligarchy is steady work—our work

Ideas have power—as long as they are not frozen in doctrine—but they need legs. The eight-hour day; the minimum wage; the conservation of natural resources and the protection of our air, water, and land; women's rights and civil rights; free trade unions; Social Security; a civil service based on merit—all these were launched as citizens' movements and won the endorsement of the political class only after long struggles and in the face of bitter opposition and sneering attacks. Democracy doesn't work without citizen activism and participation. Trickle-down politics is no more effective than trickle-down economics. Moreover, civilization happens because we don't leave things to other people. What's right and good doesn't come naturally. You have to stand up and fight as if the cause depends on you. Allow yourself that conceit—to believe that the flame of democracy will never go out as long as there's one candle in one citizen's hand.

Port Huron Statement

TOM HAYDEN

INTRODUCTION: AGENDA FOR A GENERATION

We are people of this generation, bred in at least modest comfort, housed now in universities, looking uncomfortably to the world we inherit.

When we were kids the United States was the wealthiest and strongest country in the world; the only one with the atom bomb, the least scarred by modern war, an initiator of the United Nations that we thought would distribute Western influence throughout the world. Freedom and equality for each individual, government of, by, and for the people—these American values we found good, principles by which we could live as men. Many of us began maturing in complacency.

As we grew, however, our comfort was penetrated by events too troubling to dismiss. First, the permeating and victimizing fact of human degradation, symbolized by the Southern struggle against racial bigotry, compelled most of us from silence to activism. Second, the enclosing fact of the Cold War, symbolized by the presence of the Bomb, brought awareness that we ourselves, and our friends, and millions of abstract "others" we knew more directly because of our common peril, might die at any time. We might deliberately ignore, or avoid, or fail to feel all other human problems, but not these two, for these were too immediate and crushing in their impact, too challenging in the demand that we as individuals take the responsibility for encounter and resolution.

While these and other problems either directly oppressed us or rankled our consciences and became our own subjective concerns, we began to see complicated and disturbing paradoxes in our surrounding America. The declaration "all men are created equal . . ." rang hollow before the facts of Negro life in the South and the big cities of the North. The proclaimed peaceful intentions of the United States contradicted its economic and military investments in the Cold War status quo.

We witnessed, and continue to witness, other paradoxes. With nuclear energy whole cities can easily be powered, yet the dominant nation-states seem more

Source: "Introduction: Agenda for a Generation" from "Port Huron Statement" by Tom Hayden. Reprinted with permission of Tom Hayden.

likely to unleash destruction greater than that incurred in all wars of human history. Although our own technology is destroying old and creating new forms of social organization, men still tolerate meaningless work and idleness. While two-thirds of mankind suffers under nourishment, our own upper classes revel amidst superfluous abundance. Although world population is expected to double in forty years, the nations still tolerate anarchy as a major principle of international conduct and uncontrolled exploitation governs the sapping of the earth's physical resources. Although mankind desperately needs revolutionary leadership, America rests in national stalemate, its goals ambiguous and tradition-bound instead of informed and clear, its democratic system apathetic and manipulated rather than "of, by, and for the people."

Not only did tarnish appear on our image of American virtue, not only did disillusion occur when the hypocrisy of American ideals was discovered, but we began to sense that what we had originally seen as the American Golden Age was actually the decline of an era. The worldwide outbreak of revolution against colonialism and imperialism, the entrenchment of totalitarian states, the menace of war, overpopulation, international disorder, supertechnology—these trends were testing the tenacity of our own commitment to democracy and freedom and our abilities to visualize their application to a world in upheaval.

Our work is guided by the sense that we may be the last generation in the experiment with living. But we are a minority—the vast majority of our people regard the temporary equilibriums of our society and world as eternally functional parts. In this is perhaps the outstanding paradox; we ourselves are imbued with urgency, yet the message of our society is that there is no viable alternative to the present. Beneath the reassuring tones of the politicians, beneath the common opinion that America will "muddle through," beneath the stagnation of those who have closed their minds to the future, is the pervading feeling that there simply are no alternatives, that our times have witnessed the exhaustion not only of Utopias, but of any new departures as well. Feeling the press of complexity upon the emptiness of life, people are fearful of the thought that at any moment things might be thrust out of control. They fear change itself, since change might smash whatever invisible framework seems to hold back chaos for them now. For most Americans, all crusades are suspect, threatening. The fact that each individual sees apathy in his fellows perpetuates the common reluctance to organize for change. The dominant institutions are complex enough to blunt the minds of their potential critics, and entrenched enough to swiftly dissipate or entirely repel the energies of protest and reform, thus limiting human expectancies. Then, too, we are a materially improved society, and by our own improvements we seem to have weakened the case for further change.

Some would have us believe that Americans feel contentment amidst prosperity—but might it not better be called a glaze above deeply felt anxieties about their role in the new world? And if these anxieties produce a developed indifference to human affairs, do they not as well produce a yearning to believe that there is an alternative to the present, that something can be done to change circumstances in the school, the workplaces, the bureaucracies, the government? It is to this latter yearning, at once the spark and engine of change, that we direct our present appeal. The search for truly democratic alternatives to the present, and a commitment to social experimentation with them, is a worthy and fulfilling human enterprise, one which moves us and, we hope, others today. On such a basis do we offer this document of our convictions and analysis: as an effort in understanding and changing the conditions of humanity in the late twentieth century, an effort rooted in the ancient, still unfulfilled conception of man attaining determining influence over his circumstances of life.

VALUES

Making values explicit—an initial task in establishing alternatives—is an activity that has been devalued and corrupted. The conventional moral terms of the age, the politician moralities—"free world," "people's democracies"—reflect realities poorly, if at all, and seem to function more as ruling myths than as descriptive principles. But neither has our experience in the universities brought us moral enlightenment. Our professors and administrators sacrifice controversy to public relations; their curriculums change more slowly than the living events of the world; their skills and silence are purchased by investors in the arms race; passion is called unscholastic. The questions we might want raised—what is really important? can we live in a different and better way? if we wanted to change society, how would we do it?—are not thought to be questions of a "fruitful, empirical nature," and thus are brushed aside.

   Unlike youth in other countries we are used to moral leadership being exercised and moral dimensions being clarified by our elders. But today, for us, not even the liberal and socialist preachments of the past seem adequate to the forms of the present. Consider the old slogans: Capitalism Cannot Reform Itself, United Front Against Fascism, General Strike, All Out on May Day. Or, more recently, No Cooperation with Commies and Fellow Travelers, Ideologies Are Exhausted, Bipartisanship, No Utopias. These are incomplete, and there are few new prophets. It has been said that our liberal and socialist predecessors were plagued by vision without program, while our own generation is plagued by program without vision. All around us there is astute grasp of method, technique—the committee, the ad hoc group, the lobbyist, the hard and soft sell, the make, the projected image—but, if pressed critically, such expertise is incompetent to explain its implicit ideals. It is highly fashionable to identify oneself by old categories, or by naming a respected political figure, or by explaining "how we would vote" on various issues.

   Theoretic chaos has replaced the idealistic thinking of old—and, unable to reconstitute theoretic order, men have condemned idealism itself. Doubt has replaced hopefulness—and men act out a defeatism that is labeled realistic. The decline of utopia and hope is in fact one of the defining features of social life today. The reasons are various: the dreams of the older left were perverted by Stalinism and never re-created; the congressional stalemate makes men narrow their view of the possible; the specialization of human activity leaves little room for sweeping thought; the horrors of the twentieth century symbolized in the gas ovens and concentration camps and atom bombs, have blasted hopefulness. To be idealistic is to be considered apocalyptic, deluded. To have no serious aspirations, on the contrary, is to be "tough-minded."

In suggesting social goals and values, therefore, we are aware of entering a sphere of some disrepute. Perhaps matured by the past, we have no formulas, no closed theories—but that does not mean values are beyond discussion and tentative determination. A first task of any social movement is to convince people that the search for orienting theories and the creation of human values is complex but worthwhile. We are aware that to avoid platitudes we must analyze the concrete conditions of social order. But to direct such an analysis we must use the guideposts of basic principles. Our own social values involve conceptions of human beings, human relationships, and social systems.

We regard men as infinitely precious and possessed of unfulfilled capacities for reason, freedom, and love. In affirming these principles we are aware of countering perhaps the dominant conceptions of man in the twentieth century: that he is a thing to be manipulated, and that he is inherently incapable of directing his own affairs. We oppose the depersonalization that reduces human being to the status of things— if anything, the brutalities of the twentieth century teach that means and ends are intimately related, that vague appeals to "posterity" cannot justify the mutilations of the present. We oppose, too, the doctrine of human incompetence because it rests essentially on the modern fact that men have been "competently" manipulated into incompetence—we see little reason why men cannot meet with increasing the skill the complexities and responsibilities of their situation, if society is organized not for minority, but for majority, participation in decision-making.

Men have unrealized potential for self-cultivation, self-direction, self-understanding, and creativity. It is this potential that we regard as crucial and to which we appeal, not to the human potentiality for violence, unreason, and submission to authority. The goal of man and society should be human independence: a concern not with image of popularity but with finding a meaning in life that is personally authentic; a quality of mind not compulsively driven by a sense of powerlessness, nor one which unthinkingly adopts status values, nor one which represses all threats to its habits, but one which has full, spontaneous access to present and past experiences, one which easily unites the fragmented parts of personal history, one which openly faces problems which are troubling and unresolved; one with an intuitive awareness of possibilities, an active sense of curiosity, an ability and willingness to learn.

This kind of independence does not mean egotistic individualism—the object is not to have one's way so much as it is to have a way that is one's own. Nor do we deify man—we merely have faith in his potential.

Human relationships should involve fraternity and honesty. Human interdependence is contemporary fact; human brotherhood must be willed, however, as a condition of future survival and as the most appropriate form of social relations. Personal links between man and man are needed, especially to go beyond the partial and fragmentary bonds of function that bind men only as worker to worker, employer to employee, teacher to student, American to Russian.

Loneliness, estrangement, isolation describe the vast distance between man and man today. These dominant tendencies cannot be overcome by better personnel management, nor by improved gadgets, but only when a love of man overcomes the idolatrous worship of things by man. As the individualism we affirm is not egoism, the selflessness we affirm is not self-elimination. On the contrary, we believe in generosity of a kind that imprints one's unique individual qualities in the relation to other men, and to all human activity. Further, to dislike isolation is not to favor the abolition of privacy; the latter differs from isolation in that it occurs or is abolished according to individual will.

We would replace power rooted in possession, privilege, or circumstance by power and uniqueness rooted in love, reflectiveness, reason, and creativity. As a social system we seek the establishment of a democracy of individual participation, governed by two central aims: that the individual share in those social decisions determining the quality and direction of his life; that society be organized to encourage independence in men and provide the media for their common participation.

> In a participatory democracy, the political life would be based in several root principles: that decision-making of basic social consequence be carried on by public groupings;
>
> that politics be seen positively, as the art of collectively creating an acceptable pattern of social relations;
>
> that politics has the function of bringing people out of isolation and into community, thus being a necessary, though not sufficient, means of finding meaning in personal life;
>
> that the political order should serve to clarify problems in a way instrumental to their solution; it should provide outlets for the expression of personal grievance and aspiration; opposing views should be organized so as to illuminate choices and facilitate the attainment of goals; channels should be commonly available to relate men to knowledge and to power so that private problems—from bad recreation facilities to personal alienation—are formulated as general issues.

The economic sphere would have as its basis the principles:

> that work should involve incentives worthier than money or survival. It should be educative, not stultifying; creative, not mechanical; self-directed, not manipulated, encouraging independence, a respect for others, a sense of dignity, and a willingness to accept social responsibility, since it is this experience that has crucial influence on habits, perceptions and individual ethics;
>
> that the economic experience is so personally decisive that the individual must share in its full determination;
>
> that the economy itself is of such social importance that its major resources and means of production should be open to democratic participation and subject to democratic social regulation.

Like the political and economic ones, major social institutions—cultural, educational, rehabilitative, and others—should be generally organized with the well-being and dignity of man as the essential measure of success.

In social change or interchange, we find violence to be abhorrent because it requires generally the transformation of the target, be it a human being or a community of people, into a depersonalized object of hate. It is imperative that the means of violence be abolished and the institutions—local, national, international—that encourage non-violence as a condition of conflict be developed.

These are our central values, in skeletal form. It remains vital to understand their denial or attainment in the context of the modern world.

_____ADDITIONAL READINGS_____

Broesamle, John, and Anthony Arthur. 2005. *Clashes of Will: Great Confrontations That Have Shaped Modern America.* New York: Pearson Longman.

This book is about the clashing ideas that involved social movements such as race and gender equality, the rights of workers, and social welfare.

Marabel, Manning. 2005. *W. E. B. Du Bois: Black Radical Democrat* (new updated edition). Boulder, CO: Paradigm.

This biography of the great African American scholar and activist W. E. B. Du Bois chronicles the struggles against Jim Crow segregation and his contributions toward racial equality.

Young, Ralph F. 2005. *Dissent in America Since 1865,* Volume II. New York: Longman.

An anthology of original essays, speeches, and manifestos that were the rallying cries for movements aimed at establishing the goals of democracy for the poor, workers, racial minorities, and women.

Zinn, Howard. 1997. *The Zinn Reader: Writings on Disobedience and Democracy.* New York: Seven Stories Press.

The compiled writings of radical historian Howard Zinn provide the rationales for movements advancing civil rights, peace, and voting rights.

CHAPTER 4

Social Movements Promoting Corporate Social Responsibility

Large-scale corporations have achieved immense power and influence in these times of rapidly expanding global economic activity and trade. Sociologists like G. William Domhoff have established that government in the United States has favored the interests of corporate enterprises since the beginning of the nation, but never has this been more true than now. Corporations enjoy low tax rates, diminishing influence from opposing groups such as labor unions, numerous government subsidies, and a permanent place at the table whenever government policies that affect even their most remote interests are considered, fashioned, or decided.

Economic conservatives believe that corporate power is a good thing because corporations generally act in ways that are in everyone's best interests by creating jobs, new technologies, and new markets. Thus, conservatives argue corporations should be guided by the marketplace, not government intervention. Political progressives, on the other hand, argue that corporations also engage in marketing schemes to keep prices artificially high, price gouging, and sometimes even strategies to defraud stockholders. Seen in this light, government agencies need to watch over corporations. Also, there is the perception by many that corporate power is heartless because profits supersede people. This is seen in outsourcing, downsizing, union busting, and in the blackmailing of communities for tax breaks. In this context, some Americans have joined with others to challenge corporations to keep their actions within the bounds of social responsibility. This chapter records the efforts of five such social movements. Their stories are worthy. They show some of the ways that the immense and growing power of corporations can be checked from the grassroots up.

The chapter begins by updating the inspiring story of college students who in the late 1990s effectively challenged the sweatshop labor practices of international companies like Nike, GAP, and others in the global apparel industry. The anti-sweatshop movement of the 1990s surprised many people because the "conventional wisdom" of the time held that American youth were morally indifferent to the plight of persons other than themselves. For many years leading up even to the present day, national surveys of entering college freshmen (conducted each year at UCLA) show that students are more interested in college education that helps them to be financially secure, and less interested in careers that make meaningful contributions to others. Yet, when thousands of students learned in the 1990s that the caps and T-shirts sold to them to express college pride were actually produced under sweatshop and slavelike conditions by workers all over the world—including many children—they took a stand.

Under pressure from students, hundreds of college and university administrations across the nation adopted new "ethical" purchasing practices in the late 1990s. The new practices that students promoted got schools to join with the Worker's Rights Consortium (an organization created by students, university administrators, and labor experts) and with the giant international corporations that supply college apparel to athletic teams, bookstores, and other outlets. The goal was to create a mechanism to monitor labor practices in factories throughout the world to ensure elimination of sweatshop abuses. This "Sweat-Free Campus Campaign" of students against the global apparel industry continues to gain support on U.S. campuses today, and the movement has spread to colleges in other nations as well.

But the movement of students against sweatshops also has expanded horizons since the beginnings in the 1990s. For example, student groups at the University of North Carolina, the University of Tennessee, and Washington University in St. Louis have recently noticed that the schools themselves are outsourcing jobs in such areas as food service and janitorial work to low-cost contractors who often pay workers sub-par wages. The students protested to pressure the universities to ensure "living wage" standards and benefits to these workers, and a broader network of students against sweatshops is working to attract students on other campuses into the fray.

In the first article, Michael Blanding gives the details on another new front where students against oppressive labor conditions are working to hold corporations socially responsible. Students are discovering global businesses other than the apparel industry that reap huge profits from routine contracts with schools and colleges. One such business is Coca-Cola. Just think of all the vending machines that are installed on your campus. Who checks on the global labor practices of the giant Coca-Cola corporation? Students do! Blanding's article discusses this.

In the 1830s, just five decades after the founding of the American nation, a French intellectual named Alexis de Toqueville visited the United States trying to discover the secrets for the success of U.S. democracy. Among the many notable observations Toqueville made was that the people in the United States were more free than in other nations to organize and assert their local interests in the form of citizens' movements. Citizens' social movements have a long history of bottom up impact in America, and the second selection in this chapter shows that this continues. Author Adam Sacks tells the story of rural Pennsylvania citizens who took on large-scale corporate farming operators seeking to transform their agricultural communities in recent years. In the process of organizing against corporate farming interests, Sacks shows how rural Pennsylvania citizens learned deep and lasting lessons about the meaning of democracy in the United States.

The third article in this section also features the bottom up power of citizens' movements from a different angle. Since Toqueville's visit to the United States, a whole range of citizens' advocacy groups have organized to counter numerous corporate special interest groups. Organizations like the American Civil Liberties Union (ACLU) and the Sierra Club are examples. The Association of Community Organizations for Reform Now (ACORN) is perhaps lesser known than the ACLU or the Sierra Club. But author David Swanson recounts how ACORN organized home mortgage borrowers nationwide against the predatory lending practices of one lender, Household International. The efforts of ACORN impacted the whole of the mortgage lending industry for the common good.

A final theme in this chapter concerns the labor movement in the United States. Next to the civil rights movement of the 1960s and 1970s, there is probably no other bottom up social movement in U.S. history that has had more important impacts on the nation than the labor movement. In recent decades, however, the influence of the labor movement has declined, as the membership in unions declined from over 30 percent of workers in the 1950s to a little over ten percent today. Although opponents of the labor movement have celebrated this decline, this chapter shows that the bottom up influence of the labor movement in the United States is not finished. The last two articles demonstrate this. Unions are experimenting these days for new ways of representing the workers from the bottom up. Author Ricky Baldwin tells how a union of tomato pickers (the Coalition of Immokalee Workers, or CIW) used a strategy they call "community unionism" to force Yum! Brands (the owner of Taco Bell and one the world's largest restaurant corporations) to deal more fairly with the poor labor conditions of immigrant farmworkers in Florida. The last article by Amy Joyce details another union reorganization experiment. Joyce tells how the United Food and Commercial Workers (UFCW), after years of trying traditional union methods to organize Wal-Mart's workers (Wal-Mart is the single largest private employer of U.S. workers and notoriously anti-union), hired a group of political campaign experts to launch an Internet-based media campaign aimed at tarnishing and shaming Wal-Mart's brand name with true but unseemly stories about the company's unfair labor practices. Corporations like Wal-Mart spend billions building themes like "Always low prices." Labor advocates are learning to fight back by shaming these themes.

Coke: The New Nike

MICHAEL BLANDING

Ever since its "I'd like to teach the world to sing" commercials from the 1970s, Coca-Cola has billed itself as the world's beverage, uniting all colors and cultures within its red-and-white swoosh. Behind that image, however, a growing student movement is taking the company to task for its less than harmonious record of human rights around the globe.

Chief among the accusations is the company's alleged complicity in the murder of union members by paramilitaries at bottling plants in Colombia. So far, six colleges and universities in the United States—including Carleton, Oberlin and Bard—have responded to a call by the Colombian beverages union for a boycott, either by canceling contracts or banning vending machines. Campaigns are active at about ninety more, making this the largest anticorporate campaign since the one against Nike. "Coke sells an image," says Camilo Romero, a national organizer with United Students Against Sweatshops. "As with any campaign like this, it is hurting its image that will hurt their bottom line."

Romero says that in addition to boycotts, students will soon be conducting sit-ins similar to those that helped publicize sweatshop abuses by Nike and other companies in the late 1990s. That campaign had mixed results; Nike eventually disclosed the locations of its factories and raised wages slightly but failed to follow through on other promises to monitor abuses. More recently, a student campaign helped contribute to a victory against Taco Bell by migrant workers fighting to raise the prices paid to them for tomatoes they picked.

Fresh from that success, Romero appeared last month before a packed auditorium at Smith College, where the administration has so far responded favorably to student calls for a Coke boycott. With him was Javier Correa, president of the Colombian union SINALTRAINAL, who spoke of a decade of violence that has resulted in the deaths of eight workers. As an example, he told the story of Isidro Gil, who was shot dead in 1996 at the bottling plant; a week

Source: "Coke: The New Nike" by Michael Blanding. Reprinted with permission from the March 24, 2005 issue of *The Nation*. For subscription information, call 1-800-333-8536. Portions of each week's Nation magazine can be accessed at www.thenation.com.

later, paramilitaries entered the plant and forced workers to sign letters of resig-
nation from the union at gunpoint. Coca-Cola directly controls the bottling facilities through their contracts, said Correa, who says he has himself escaped three
assassination attempts. "It's clear they have the power to stop what's happening."

In an e-mail, Coke's issues director, Lori George Billingsley, denies that the
companies or its bottlers have been involved in the violence. "We are disappointed
in the student boycotts because the campaigns are based on inaccuracies regarding the situation on the ground," she writes. The company recently announced that
it will be conducting audits of worker conditions around the world, but it has
stopped short of agreeing to demands for an independent investigation into the
murders. "They are trying to deal with these ugly allegations as a public relations
matter rather then the serious matter they are," says Ray Rogers, head of the Killer
Coke Campaign, which is helping to direct the student boycotts.

The campaign has rattled Coke, which has dispatched representatives from
its headquarters in Atlanta and from its subsidiary in Colombia to campuses to
argue its case. At New York University, a heated debate between Billingsley and
students preceded a vote by the University Committee on Student Life in December approving the boycott. This month, however, that decision was overturned by
the university senate, which opted instead for a letter to the company urging it to
agree to an investigation, requesting a response by April 20. The softer measure
was denounced by the college newspaper as thwarting the will of the students,
some of whom have vowed more direct action.

Despite NYU's high profile, two large universities with long-term Coke
contracts may hold more influence over whether the campaign succeeds. The
51,000-student Rutgers University in New Jersey recently held a public hearing
at which student after student stood up to demand cancellation of the university's
ten-year, $10 million exclusive beverages contact. A committee of faculty, staff,
and students will make the final decision before the contract expires at the end
of May.

At the 39,000-student University of Michigan, the Coke case will be the first
test of a new university policy to hold its vendors accountable to a code of
conduct that includes human rights. As with the case at NYU, the university's
student assembly passed a resolution supporting the campaign's allegations. The
final decision on whether to cancel the university's contracts—collectively worth
about $1.3 million a year—now falls to a student-faculty dispute review board,
which plans a ruling before the first contract expires in June.

Significantly, the campaign at Michigan has expanded the charges beyond
the allegations in Colombia to include human rights abuses in India, where the
company has been accused of causing drought and pollution that has hurt farmers.
"What's happening in both Colombia and India are proximate causes," says
junior Ryan Bates. "There is an underlying flaw in the global trade structure that
puts values of for-profit corporations over values of people and communities.

"Reflecting a trend in the anticorporate globalization movement to draw connections between disparate issues, other groups adding their voices to the campaign are accusing Coke of child labor in El Salvador, failure to provide healthcare for workers with HIV/AIDS in Africa and even childhood obesity in the United States.

Meanwhile, the university campaign continues to grow internationally, with three colleges in Ireland, one in Italy, and one in Canada joining the boycott. Rogers says that colleges are now contacting him to say they've started campaigns. His next target: vending machines in high schools. "Coke would have to hire an army of people to respond to all of the fires that we've got going," he says.

Rights Fight:
Townships in Rural Pennsylvania Take on Factory Farms—and Corporate Rights

ADAM D. SACKS

In the late 1990s, life was getting tough for agribusiness in North Carolina. Over the previous decade or so, the state had risen from the number 15 hog producer in the country to number two. With more hogs than people North Carolina's largely African-American Duplin and Sampson counties were the two largest pork-producing counties in the nation. By 1997, pollution, public health, and environmental justice problems were causing such widespread outcry that the state imposed a moratorium on all new pig farms that would last for almost six years. Soon factory farm corporations went on the prowl for greener pastures, so to speak.

Central Pennsylvania looked like an attractive target. It has an excellent system of roadways and accessible distribution centers. Land is relatively cheap. Many small farmers were, as usual, struggling. The Pennsylvania Farm Bureau, nominally a farmer advocacy organization, is firmly in the pocket of big agribusiness and highly influential in the state legislature. The central part of the state is rural, with township populations ranging from several hundred to a few thousand. This means there were no zoning regulations—the townships didn't think they needed them—to get in the way of large-scale hog farming. Rural township governments had no idea how to deal with powerful businesses. In short, the townships between Philadelphia in the east and Pittsburgh in the west were sitting ducks. Or so the ag boys thought.

ONSLAUGHT

The phone was ringing off the hook in the office of Thomas Linzey, a young attorney at the nonprofit organization he founded, the Community Environmental

Source: "Rights Fight" by Adam D. Sacks, *Dollars and Sense,* #260, July/August 2005, pp. 21–24. Reprinted with permission of Adam D. Sacks, Executive Director, Center for Democracy and the Constitution.

Legal Defense Fund (CELDF). Three years out of law school, Linzey was one of a rare breed of lawyers dedicated full time to public interest law. Idealistic and determined, he had set up a regulatory practice to help communities appeal permits issued to businesses they didn't want in their backyards. And he was good at it. In hearing after hearing, he pointed out defects in permit applications and convinced regulators and judges that these irresponsible corporate entities shouldn't be allowed to ply their noxious trades. Permits were rescinded, communities celebrated victories, Linzey and CELDF won prizes and kudos and were invited to Environment Day at the White House as guests of Vice President Al Gore. But there was a problem.

A few months after a community victory, the heretofore unpermitted corporation would return, permit in hand, ready to do business. What had happened? The only relevant issue in the regulatory appeal, whether all the bureaucratic dotted i's and crossed t's were in place, was resolved: the community had unearthed the problems with the permit, and the corporation proceeded to fix them. By challenging the permit and exposing the defects, the community had unwittingly done the corporation's work for free. Since townships of a few thousand people generally don't stand much of a chance against corporate legal budgets, practically speaking there was no further recourse.

Linzey had been puzzling over the battles won and wars lost in his first three years when the factory farm onslaught began. Local township officials, farmers, and concerned citizens were calling him, desperate, saying, "They're telling us that all we can do is regulate manure odor—but we don't want these toxic and destructive factory farms in our community at all! Please help us figure this out."

Factory pig farm operations produce tons of manure a day, which ends up in lakes, rivers, and drinking water. They not only seriously damage the environment—they also wreak havoc on the local economy and put independent family farmers out of business. Struggling farmers enter into one-sided output contracts with agribusiness corporations, agreeing to sell only to them. On their face, these contracts appear to be a way of guaranteeing a small farmer a market. But farmers soon find themselves trapped. The contracts hook them into expensive capital improvements that can cost hundreds of thousands of dollars, often paid for with loans issued by the corporations themselves. The contracts give the corporation ownership over all of the farm's animals—unless some die, in which case responsibility for the carcasses reverts to the farmers for disposal. And they allow the corporations to evade responsibility for environmental damage, since the giant firms don't technically own the property.

The result is an unequal arrangement in which the farmers own their land, but are so in hock to their corporate buyers, and utterly dependent on them, that they effectively lose control of their operations. The corporate party can unilaterally terminate the contract at any time, leaving the farmers to bail themselves out if they can. Most lose everything.

Like the township officials, Linzey was at a loss at first, but figured it was worth looking around to see what the possibilities were. He discovered that nine states, from Oklahoma in 1907 to South Dakota in 1998, had passed laws or constitutional amendments against corporate ownership or control of farms. Some of these laws contained exceptions for incorporated farms that were family owned and operated on a daily basis by one or more family members. That is, they didn't affect real farmers—people who wake up before sunrise, mingle with cows and pigs, and get their hands and boots dirty—but did cover the farms owned by corporate executives. Linzey converted text from these existing laws into a "Farm Ownership Ordinance" that many townships considered, and some passed. The ordinance template stated: "No corporation or syndicate may acquire, or otherwise obtain an interest, whether legal, beneficial, or otherwise, in any real estate used for farming in this Township, or engage in farming."

WHAT HAPPENED TO OUR LOCAL DEMOCRACY?

Although the citizens of rural Pennsylvania townships would be the last to call themselves activists or revolutionaries, their battles to preserve the health and integrity of their lives and homes against corporate assault have the makings of a socio-political earthquake. These mostly conservative Republican communities found themselves asking what had happened to their democracy.

How did it come to pass that a small handful of corporate directors a thousand miles away got to decide what takes place in their backyards? Why does the democratic decision of hundreds or thousands of citizens to keep out dangerous and destructive activity get trumped by distant interests whose only concern is how much of the community's wealth they can run away with, regardless of the collateral damage to the environment, economy, and social fabric of the community? As one town supervisor put it, "What the hell are rights of corporations?"

In short, the townspeople began having conversations about what it means to be a sovereign people, with inalienable rights, whose government operates only with their consent—conversations that hadn't been heard in the town commons or around kitchen tables for a long, long time. Organized by community leaders among friends and neighbors who had never before been active in civic affairs, their meetings took various forms. There were formal county-wide gatherings of hundreds of people, small conclaves in living rooms, and backyard barbecue chats. Armed with copies of the Constitution and Declaration of Independence, they asked and tried to answer basic questions, such as: What is a democracy? What are the people's rights, responsibilities, and privileges? What is the law? Who makes it and who enforces it? What are the courts? Whose side are they on?

Citizens realized that the issue was not really the factory farm or the sludged field. The issue was who has the right to decide what happens in our communities: we the people, or the corporations that have taken over our economy and our government for the benefit of the very few to the detriment of the rest of us. Farms are just one of a thousand different fronts to fight harms from pollution to corruption to war. But after all, in a democracy—and perhaps in human society in general—there's only one fundamental issue from which all governing process derives: the right to decide.

People in many central Pennsylvania townships had these conversations. They began shunning the regulatory system and instead passed ordinances to control both factory farms and another threat that appeared at around the same time: land-applied sewage sludge (which had caused the tragic deaths of two teenagers in 1995). Seventy townships passed antisludge ordinances, which imposed a fee to render land application of sewage sludge unprofitable. They remain sludge-free. Eleven townships passed factory farm ordinances, which outlawed nonfamily corporate ownership and control of farming operations. None has a factory farm to date. Two townships, Licking and Porter, even passed ordinances stripping corporations of their constitutional rights outright. Within their towns, corporations would no longer have the status of "persons."

All of this exercise of local control began to cause some serious discomfort among agribusiness interests. Of course, corporations could go ahead and sue the townships, which they did, claiming that their constitutional rights as legal persons had been abrogated. Such outrageous but judicially and legislatively supported claims infuriated the people in targeted communities: citizen response to the corporate claim of personhood became a crucial component in the subsequent organizing. But soon corporations were pursuing a more efficient tactic than lawsuits. It involved having elected officials do their heavy lifting.

POLITICAL BLOWBACK

On May 2, 2001, Pennsylvania Senate Bill 826 was filed with the Agriculture and Rural Affairs Committee. Couched as an amendment to a 1982 act protecting agricultural operations from nuisance suits and ordinances under certain circumstances, the bill aimed to crack down on township efforts. The amendment further limited the ability of localities to pass ordinances, and it wasn't the least bit subtle, reading: "No municipality shall adopt or enact a frivolous ordinance that would prohibit, restrict, or regulate an agricultural operation." What counts as "frivolous"? Any attempt to "regulate the type of business that may own or conduct an agricultural operation." Just to drive home the point and punish any township that tried to protect itself, the bill entitles the aggrieved party to recover costs and attorney fees from lawsuits they file to challenge the ordinances.

When Linzey heard about 826, he set out to rally the people. An unprecedented coalition formed to oppose this assault on local democracy. The Sierra Club, the United Mine Workers of America, Common Cause, the Pennsylvania

Farmers Union, the Pennsylvania Association for Sustainable Agriculture, and 400 rural township governments all joined to defeat 826. Groups that ordinarily wouldn't be talking to each other found common ground not because they were fighting sewage sludge or factory farms or some other single issue, but because they could all agree that the state was out of bounds in usurping basic democratic rights. Senate Bill 826 never made it out of committee.

But it wasn't over yet. In one of those dark backrooms of the statehouse where corporate politics thrive, the bill was renumbered, and on May 2, 2002, it was slipped back into the Senate, where it passed 48 to 2. A leaked Pennsylvania Farm Bureau memorandum said that the renumbering was necessary to avoid any bad publicity. People told Linzey, "Nice try—but you'll never win against a vote like that." Undaunted, the coalition stormed into action, and threatened enough legislators with loss of a job that the bill never came to a vote in the House.

And it still wasn't over—illustrating the Jeffersonian wisdom that the price of liberty is constant vigilance.

This time, in 2003, the agribusiness forces attached the substance of the bill to an anti-sexual predator law on the last day of the legislative session. They figured that in an election year no legislator would want to be vulnerable to charges of favoring molesting children (although the freshman sponsor of that bill withdrew her sponsorship, saying that the bill was intended to protect children, not corporations). As soon as the bill landed on the desk of Democratic Governor Ed Rendell, the local democracy forces barraged him. He backed down and didn't sign the bill, but explained that this was only because better top-down regulatory protection was in order. With better state rules, he implied, it would be okay to strip municipalities of their rights.

In 2004, Rendell unveiled his ACRE initiative (Agriculture, Communities, and Rural Environment), under which an appointed political board would have the authority to overturn local laws. In other words, laws passed democratically by a majority of citizens in a community could be struck down by an unelected collection of corporate appointees. The coalition has beat that one back too for now—it will likely come up again in the next legislative session.

So the vigilance continues. Each time the state government attempts such probusiness shenanigans, it increasingly reveals on whose behalf it is working. And each time, more people see with growing clarity how relentlessly their lives and rights are sold and legislated away, and begin to understand how the failure of democracy leads to very real harms in their communities.

There is broader significance to such fights to save the sustainable family farm. It's about the underlying political power structure and its links to economic power. It's about who decides the fate of communities, and in whose interest those decisions are made. Just as past empires established colonies—including those that rebelled to form our nation—for the purposes of expropriating resources to feed and entertain the nobility and the rising merchant class, so today do corporate-driven governments sustain a culture of expropriation of the commons, with a blindness and ferocity that threatens to render the earth unlivable.

Saving the sustainable family farm is also about uniting all of us who are fighting important single issue battles. As long as we are divided and scattering our energies in a thousand different directions, we will continue to lose. When we finally unite on the common terra firma of local control over sustainability, health, well-being, and democracy, we will be in a position to create an irresistible force.

Flame-Broiled Shark: ACORN's Fight to Stop Predatory Lending

DAVID SWANSON

If someone told you that a bunch of low-income people, most of them African-American or Latino, most of them women, most of them elderly, had been victimized by a predatory mortgage lender that stripped them of much of their equity or of their entire homes, you might not be surprised. But if I told you that these women and men had gotten together and, after three years of work, brought the nation's largest high-cost lender to its knees, forced it to sell out to a foreign company, and won back a half a billion dollars of what had been taken from them—one of the largest consumer settlements ever—you'd probably ask me what country this had happened in. Surely it couldn't have been in the United States of the Second Gilded Age, the land of unbridled corporate power and radical government activism on behalf of the rich and the greedy.

Yet, it was. These victims identified a problem and named it "predatory lending" in the late 1990s. Their campaign to reform Household International (also known as Household Finance and as Beneficial) played out from 2001 to 2003, concluding with a settlement that includes a ban on bad-mouthing the company. That's why more people haven't heard about this. The families who fought back and defeated Household are barred from bragging about it or teaching the lessons they learned, because that would require recounting the damage that Household did to homes and neighborhoods. These families are members of ACORN, the Association of Community Organizations for Reform Now.

I was ACORN's communications coordinator during much of the Household campaign, but left before it ended. No one has asked me not to tell this story.

In low-income minority neighborhoods in the United States, what little wealth there is, is in home equity. Home equity makes up 74.9 percent of the net wealth for Hispanics in the bottom two income quintiles (0-40 percent) and 78.7 percent of the net wealth for African Americans in the second income quintile

Source: "Flame-Broiled Shark" by David Swanson, *Z Magazine*, May 2005, Vol. 18, #5, pp. 30–32. Reprinted by permission of David Swanson.

(20-40 percent). There have been gains in minority home ownership over the past few decades, in part as a result of the work by community groups like ACORN and National People's Action to force banks to make loans in these communities, but the home ownership is fragile and not protected by additional savings. Lenders in the past decade have focused on stripping away equity and community groups have been forced to focus on keeping out loans that are worse than no loans at all.

Most high-cost loans are refinance loans. Too often they are marketed aggressively and deceptively, including through live-checks in the mail that result in very high-cost loans that the lender will be only too happy to refinance into a new mortgage. Often these loans are made with excessive, sometimes variable, interest rates, outrageously high fees, and fees financed into the loans so that the borrower pays interest on them and often is not told about them. They are made with bogus products built in, on which the borrower also pays interest. Hidden balloon payments force repeated refinancings for additional fees each time. Mandatory arbitration clauses attempt to prevent borrowers from taking lenders to court. The practice of loaning more than the value of a home traps borrowers in loans they cannot refinance with a responsible lender. Consolidation of additional debts further decreases equity, placing the home at greater risk. Quiet omission of taxes and insurance from a mortgage that previously included those charges results in a crisis when yearly bills arrive.

Predatory lenders turn the usual logic of lending upside down. They make their money by intentionally making loans that the borrowers will be unable to repay. They charge fees for each refinancing until finally seizing the house. Fannie Mae has estimated that as many as half of all borrowers in subprime (high-cost) loans could have qualified for a lower cost mortgage.

High-cost loans are not just made to people with poor credit. They're often made to people who have poor banking services in their neighborhoods.

ACORN members don't take abuse of their neighborhoods lying down, and Household was a leading cause of the rows of vacant houses appearing in ACORN neighborhoods in the 1990s. ACORN launched a campaign to reform Household that included numerous strategies. One, an ACORN stand-by, was direct action. Repeatedly, ACORN members in numerous cities around the country simultaneously protested in Household offices to demand reform. At the same time, ACORN was working to pass anti-predatory lending legislation in local and state governments and Congress. ACORN members made sure that in each case the victims testifying were victims of Household and that Household's abuses were highlighted. When ACORN released major reports on predatory lending, the examples included were always from Household.

ACORN also worked with the Coalition for Responsible Wealth to advance a shareholder resolution that would have tied Household's executives' compensation to ending its predatory lending. In 2001 Household held its shareholders meeting in an out-of-the-way suburb of Tampa, Florida. A crowd of ACORN members was there with shark suits and shark balloons to protest.

The resolution won [only] 5 percent [of the vote]. Over the next year, ACORN pressured state pension funds and other shareholders. Household held its 2002 meeting an hour and a half from the nearest airport in rural Kentucky. Members made the trip by car from all over the country. The protest may have been the biggest thing the town of London, Kentucky had seen in years. The resolution won [just] 30 percent [of the vote].

As a result, various local and state governments threatened to divest from Household. ACORN also put pressure on stores like Best Buy that used Household credit cards. At the same time, ACORN Housing Corporation was assisting many Household victims in either refinancing out of their Household loans or at least canceling some of the rip-off services built into their loans, such as credit insurance. ACORN was getting the word out to stay away from Household.

ACORN wrote up numerous accounts of Household predatory loans and took them to the attorney generals in state after state urging investigations. ACORN similarly pressured federal regulators to act. ACORN assisted borrowers in filing a number of class-action suits against Household targeting those of its practices that were clearly illegal even under existing law. They let Wall Street analysts know what Household stood to lose from these lawsuits, as well as from various reforms that Household periodically announced in its attempt to hold off the pressure.

But ACORN members never let up. They protested again and again at Household offices and held press conferences in front of homes about to be lost to Household. They protested the secondary market that was putting up capital for these predatory loans and they held a major protest at the trade group that lobbied in Washington for Household and its fellow sharks. Then, in the summer of 2002, in the wealthy suburbs north of Chicago, victims of Household from around the country poured out of busses by the thousands onto the lawns of the board members and the CEO of Household. They knocked on doors and spoke to those who had hurt them from a distance. When the police made them leave, ACORN members plastered "Wanted" posters all over the neighborhood telling the board members' neighbors what crimes the Household executives were guilty of.

Through all of this, we worked the media. I kept a database of victims' stories and contact information and put them in touch with reporters whenever the reporters were willing to tell not just the victimization story, but also the story of fighting back. We generated several hundred print articles and several hundred TV and radio stories about Household's predatory lending practices. We worked the small neighborhood papers, flyers in churches, posters on walls. We provoked lengthy articles in the *New York Times, Washington Post, Wall Street Journal, Los Angeles Times*, and *Forbes Magazine*. We kept up an endless barrage in the trade press: the *American Banker, National Mortgage News*, etc.

A handful of ACORN staff people with great expertise and unrelenting effort organized thousands of members to drive this campaign until Household agreed to pay victims $489 million through the 50 states attorneys general, and later agreed to pay millions more through ACORN, as well as to reform its practices.

This campaign was an example of what can be done if enough different angles are pursued at once and the company ripping you off is put on the defensive and constantly hit with the unexpected. This campaign increased the size and power of ACORN to effect future progressive change. This is good news for low-income neighborhoods, but bad news for Wells Fargo, the predatory lender who is next on ACORN's list.

Tomato Pickers Win Big at Taco Bell

RICKY BALDWIN

Amid jubilant tears and hugs, Florida tomato pickers announced March 8, 2005 that they had defeated all the odds, and considerable corporate inertia, to win a clear victory in the first-ever farmworker boycott campaign against a major fast food restaurant chain, Taco Bell. Based in Immokalee, Florida, the Coalition of Immokalee Workers (CIW) represents some of the poorest, most abused workers in the U.S.

Taco Bell is owned by the single largest restaurant corporation in the world, Yum! Brands. After years of protest, the restaurant "mega-firm" finally agreed to pay an extra penny a pound for its tomatoes and to buy only from suppliers who agree to pass along the extra "one cent for justice" to tomato pickers. Yum! also agreed to work with CIW to improve conditions in the fields and called on other restaurant firms to follow suit.

Beginning to address these working conditions, for example, the company says it will now take steps to ensure that its tomato suppliers no longer employ indentured servants, immigrant farmworkers who are locked into squalid labor camps at night until they pay off certain debts. Corporate spokespeople said the company would "eat the cost" of the agreement instead of passing the increase along to consumers. They also made it clear the agreement applies to Taco Bell alone, saying their other restaurants don't buy enough Florida tomatoes to have an impact on the market. Last year, Taco Bell purchased more than 10 million pounds of Florida tomatoes, almost one percent of the state crop.

Yum! owns over 33,000 restaurants in over 100 countries and territories, including KFC, Pizza Hut, Long John Silver's, and A&W restaurants. It employs more than 840,000 workers worldwide, making it bigger than McDonalds. Yum! grossed over $9 billion last year, just shy of McDonalds' annual revenue.

THE UNION DIFFERENCE

The farmworkers' win at Taco Bell was impressive because of the unusually precarious nature of their work. As agricultural workers, they are not covered

Source: "Tomato Pickers Win Big at Taco Bell" by Ricky Baldwin, *Z Magazine*, May 2005, Vol. 18, #5, pp. 28–30. Reprinted by permission of Ricky Baldwin.

under the 1935 National Labor Relations Act which makes it illegal for employers to fire employees for union activity, certifies union elections, and oversees collective bargaining. Nor do they enjoy the protections of other basic labor laws in the U.S., such as federal minimum wage and overtime laws.

Many U.S. farm laborers are immigrants, often undocumented, and routinely face working and living conditions that are unthinkable to most Americans. Conditions may include long hot work days, little or no access to drinking water or toilets, and beatings or other harassment. Some workers have even been held at gunpoint in the fields.

For this life, farmworkers in the U.S. generally earn about 40 cents for picking 32 pounds of tomatoes, the same rate in real terms as they earned 30 years ago. A picker has to gather fully one ton of tomatoes to earn $25.

In the late 1970s wages in the fields began a precipitous decline and continued dropping throughout the 1980s and into the 1990s. Then in 1993 a group of farm laborers in Immokalee, the largest agricultural center in Florida, began meeting in a local church to talk about how to bring about change.

Over the next few years the group organized a number of work stoppages, combined with public pressure, including three general strikes, a month-long hunger strike, and a 230-mile march from Ft. Myers to Orlando in 2000. By the end of the 1990s the Coalition of Immokalee Workers had won wage increases of 13–25 percent across the industry, not just for themselves. This series of victories ended the 20-year plummet of farmworker pay and raised wage rates back to the mid-1970's level, earning farmworker communities several million dollars a year.

Lucas Benitez, of the CIW, believes the extra penny per pound paid by Taco Bell should substantially improve the wages of about 1,000 tomato pickers employed by Taco Bell suppliers. He says that under the new agreement these workers could earn up to 72 cents for a 32-pound bucket, an increase of 80 percent. "It would mean almost reaching the poverty level," Benitez told one reporter.

OUTSIDE THE BUN

Taco Bell and its corporate owner had resisted CIW's demands for years, saying that the fast food giant was only one buyer of Florida tomatoes and that it would agree only if the rest of the industry would also pay more. In fact, as most union organizers understand, resistance to unions is rarely about the money alone.

As if to prove this, Taco Bell at one point offered to make a direct payment to CIW of $100,000, the same amount as the company's estimate of the total cost of the penny per pound "pass through." The company said they intended the payment to help CIW lobby the state legislature for protective regulations on the industry as a whole—and of course to stop the protests. CIW rejected the offer.

Taco Bell had also argued from the beginning that it was not the direct employer of the tomato pickers. This is true, but the additional point and the implication, that the chain had no control over its tomato suppliers, is not true. As a huge buyer of tomatoes, CIW argued, Taco Bell applied constant pressure on its suppliers to keep costs low, which in turn exerted downward pressure on the pickers wages. Echoing the company's own ad campaign, CIW urged Taco Bell to "think outside the bun."

It is a slogan the Immokalee Workers take to heart. Their strategies show remarkable creativity and savvy, adapting their organizing to labor markets that combine 19th century conditions with the latest innovations in capitalist globalization. Their internal egalitarianism, too, is almost unique among modern-day unions. Even Benitez, who often speaks for the group, avoids using an official title. "We are all leaders," he and others in CIW will say, when asked.

The Immokalee Workers see themselves as part of a movement, fighting for the rights of an entire community, not just their dues-paying members. Their lack of legal rights forces them to rely upon a wide variety of persuasive techniques, but what it does not force is the overcautious narrowness of purpose as in the standard union model. Theirs is a community unionism—one that wins.

The CIW strategy also seems to involve widening that community to encompass concerned individuals and groups other than farmworkers. The Taco Bell campaign reached out to churches, labor unions and student-labor networks established in the anti-sweat-shop movement. They often made this last connection explicit, calling for an end to "the sweatshops in the fields."

The student campaign hit the company where it hurt. Taco Bell's main marketing target is 18-to-24-year-olds, collectively known in the restaurant's market strategies as "The new hedonism generation." In the end, students at more than 20 high schools and colleges—including UCLA, University of Notre Dame, and the University of Chicago—organized "Boot the Bell" mini-campaigns to block or kick out on-campus Taco Bell restaurants.

CIW also works with the U.S. Department of Justice, so far forcing at least five federal prosecutions on human slavery charges, most recently involving 3 Florida citrus growers who had been holding over 700 workers in slavery. Overall, the group's website proclaims, "We have liberated over 1,000 workers."

Together with some of its allies, CIW co-founded the national Freedom Network Institute on Human Trafficking and now serves as Regional coordinator for the southeastern U.S. for the Institute. In this capacity, the group conducts trainings for law enforcement and social service personnel in identifying and assisting victims of slavery, in addition to their advocacy for full prosecution of all traffickers, both corporations and subcontractors.

This anti-slavery work continues, as does the overall fight against poverty in the fields. Both depend heavily on CIW's grass-roots organizing. Given that there is no government enforcement agency to oversee an agreement, such as the new

Taco Bell accord, for example, constant vigilance will be the price of victory. There are other buyers, too—as CIW noted before the ink was dry.

"Systemic change to ensure human rights for farmworkers is long-overdue. Taco Bell has now taken an important leadership role by securing the penny per pound pass-through from its tomato suppliers and by the other efforts it has committed to undertake to help win equal rights for farmworkers," Benitez told reporters. "But our work together is not done. Now we must convince other companies that they have the power to change the way they do business and the way workers are treated."

Benitez said the Immokalee Workers are open to future protests and boycotts to pressure other produce buyers into helping the farmworkers. "Anything is possible in this struggle," he said.

Pressuring Wal-Mart through the Use
of New Political Campaign Techniques

AMY JOYCE

It's a Thursday morning in a downtown office building on K Street. Five staffers are fielding phone calls, soliciting help, blogging and brainstorming. Handmade posters are taped to drab walls, tracking their plans and progress. White boards are scribbled on, erased and scribbled on some more. Boxes sit unpacked. Dating lives have been put on hold. There are no plans for a summer vacation. Weekend rest is fleeting.

In other words, not much has changed since these staffers were with the Howard Dean, Wesley K. Clark and John F. Kerry presidential campaigns. But this time, they are tying to win one for the Wal-Mart workers.

Their group is the latest manifestation of the ongoing campaign to change Wal-Mart Stores Inc., the nation's largest private employer. After years of failed attempts to help Wal-Mart workers organize a union, leaders of the United Food and Commercial Workers (UFCW) are trying an Internet-oriented approach developed in recent failed presidential campaigns.

When Joseph T. Hansen became president last year, he decided to switch from approaching employees inside the stores to putting on a wider campaign designed to win over the company's customers and general public. His hope is that public reaction and negative publicity will force the company's executives to change some practices.

In January, the UFCW hired 29-year-old Paul Blank, former political director of the Howard Dean presidential campaign. He pulled together a team of other young former staffers from failed Democratic presidential campaigns to start a grass-roots effort to draw in consumers. The group calls its effort Wake-Up Wal-Mart, and it tries to use tools developed in political campaigns.

Source: "Logging On with a New Campaign; Staffers Use Tactics Learned with Candidates to Pressure Wal-Mart" by Amy Joyce, *The Washington Post*, May 31, 2005. © 2005, The Washington Post, reprinted with permission.

"For a number of years, we were going by the rules," attempting to sign up workers under rights granted by the National Labor Relations Act, said William T. McDonough, head of UFCW's organizing department. "We got very frustrated."

The mega-retailer's public image had already taken some hits before the campaign began, in part because of earlier attempts by organized labor to draw attention to what it argues is the downside of Wal-Mart's dominance. Wal-Mart is facing the largest ever class-action lawsuit charging gender discrimination. Its critics say it does not pay a fair wage and creates a burden for localities because it fails to provide adequate health care for its workers. Wal-Mart has agreed to pay $11 million to settle a federal investigation that found hundreds of illegal immigrants were hired to clean its stores.

McDonough said two well-known failed organizing attempts showed that the unions had to change their tactics: Wal-Mart eliminated meatpacking positions nationwide and began to sell prepackaged meat after meatpackers at a store in Texas voted to organize in 2000. The company said it had intended to do so before the workers voted for a union. "That had a chilling impact on any other organizing," McDonough said. Wal-Mart in April closed a Jonquiere, Quebec, store where workers had voted in a union. Wal-Mart said the store was underperforming. And so the union decided to respond with a more public campaign.

"It's a very small group dealing with very big things," Blank said. Involved in politics and campaigns since he worked in Bill Bradley's office at age 12, he most recently worked for Joe Trippi, Dean's former campaign director.

The other staffers include Buffy Wicks, 27, an antiwar activist who worked on the Dean campaign and is Wake Up's political director, and Jeremy Bird, 26, who grew up in Missouri and whose mother used to work for Wal-Mart. He went to Harvard Divinity School and was a Dean campaign worker "until the bitter end."

Brendan Bush, 25, runs the group's blog. He was on the Internet crew for the Kerry campaign. "Back before I knew I was a Democrat," he said, he teased his uncle who was proud of his union membership in the Brotherhood of Locomotive Engineers and Trainmen. The group's communications adviser, Chris Kofinis, 35, helped originate the DraftWesleyClark.com campaign and was a strategist for TheNaderFactor.com, a Democratic group that worked to pull Nader voters to other candidates

Wake-Up Wal-Mart's first major action was to garner opposition to Wal-Mart for Mother's Day. The group launched a campaign called "Love Mom, Not Wal-Mart." Shoppers signed a petition promising not to buy a Mother's Day gift at the store. News of the petition went out on blogs and community activist sites. About 22,000 people signed the online promise in the week and a half before Mother's Day. Kofinis said he considered the signatures a success, not because they had an impact on Wal-Mart sales, but because he thinks they helped raise awareness of the group's criticisms of Wal-Mart.

Visitors to the organization's Web site can also enter their Zip codes to find nearby Wal-Marts and then promise, online, to take responsibility for focusing attention on that particular store. Many people signed up to do this during the Mother's Day campaign, gathering signatures for petitions criticizing Wal-Mart or standing near stores to tell people about Wal-Mart practices they dislike. "We're focusing on people who might go to Wal-Mart and don't know the facts and might change their behavior," Kofinis said.

The UFCW's membership includes employees at grocery stores, which are facing stiff competition from Wal-Mart stores, known as Supercenters, that also sell groceries.

Wal-Mart has no plans to deal with Wake-Up Wal-Mart. "We do not plan to talk with them," said Wal-Mart spokeswoman Mona Williams in an e-mail. "Some of our critics are open-minded people who are genuinely concerned about issues and want to make the world a better place. We reach out to them and try to work toward common goals. Other groups simply pull publicity stunts to further their own narrow self-interests—and Wake-Up Wal-Mart is clearly in that category."

The UFCW is not the only union pursuing a different kind of strategy. The Service Employees International Union backed a group formed earlier this year called Wal-Mart Watch. Much like Wake-Up Wal-Mart, it is trying to build alliances with other groups that disagree with Wal-Mart policies.

Some labor experts think the UFCW's different effort is long overdue. "It surprised me that it took so long for UFCW to realize it doesn't work on a store-by-store effort," said Kate L. Bronfenbrenner, director of labor education research at Cornell University in Ithaca, N.Y.

Recently, Gov. Robert L. Ehrlich Jr. vetoed a bill that would have effectively required Wal-Mart to pay more for health benefits in Maryland, and voters in a Los Angeles suburb rejected an initiative to open a Supercenter there.

Though Wal-Mart chief executive H. Lee Scott Jr. "has said he will not raise wages, if you get more stuff like the vetoed Maryland law and in Los Angeles, I think that they will begin to make some accommodations in both wages and health care," said Nelson N. Lichtenstein, editor of the upcoming book "Wal-Mart: Template for 21st Century Capitalism?" and director of the Center for the Study of Work, Labor and Democracy at the University of California at Santa Barbara.

Some believe they are seeing the beginnings of that already: Wal-Mart is launching a massive counteroffensive to protect its image. It is spending millions of dollars on advertisements in which employees praise the company as a great place to work. For the first time, Wal-Mart invited 100 journalists to its Arkansas headquarters this spring.

At a recent morning staff meeting in Wake-Up Wal-Mart's conference room, staffers poured over the clips from the day's papers and Web sites that mentioned

Wal-Mart. Many were about a supposed whistle-blower fired from the company. "Have we reached out to his lawyers?" Blank asked.

"We should get people on the Hill" who sponsored the whistle-blower legislation to respond, Kofinis said.

"We're also still getting play on this Medicaid thing, which is great," Blank continued, referring to stories about Wal-Mart workers who turned to Medicaid because they couldn't afford the company's health coverage.

His colleagues were getting antsy. Their cell phones were ringing, legs were wiggling, and the staff just wanted the morning meeting to be over so they could get back to work.

With that, Blank rallied his troops: "Trust me, they are meeting 18 hours a day to figure out what to do with us."

ADDITIONAL READINGS

Armbruster-Sandoval, Ralph. 2005. *Globalization and Cross-Border Labor Solidarity in the Americas: The Anti-Sweatshop Movement and the Struggle for Social Justice.* New York: Routledge.

Good discussion of the new alliances that students against sweatshops are making across international boundaries.

Bacon, David. 2004. *The Children of NAFTA: Labor Wars on the U.S./Mexico Border.* Berkeley: University of California Press.

In this book, the struggle of the Immokalee tomato workers is put in its proper larger context. Using the voices of farm laborers and maquila workers all caught up in the most debasing effects of NAFTA, Bacon tells their stories of unbearable poverty, repression, and struggle. Reading Bacon, one realizes how much is to be done beyond the victory of the Immokalee workers recounted in this chapter.

Clawson, Dan. 2003. *The Next Upsurge: Labor and the New Social Movements.* Ithaca, NY: Cornell University Press.

The possibilities of new labor union strategies are discussed here. Clawson sees the possible upsurge of labor unions as they fuse with global justice issues and breakdown the boundaries between traditional unions and communities, as in the Immokolee workers venture.

Esbenshade, Jill. 2004. *Monitoring Sweatshops: Workers, Consumers, and the Global Apparel Industry.* Philadelphia: Temple University Press.

The students against sweatshops movement deals with an octopus of global trade relations. Its accomplishments are bound to be limited. Here the limits of accomplishment are well discussed.

Featherstone, Liza. 2002. *Students against Sweatshops: The Making of a Movement.* New York: Verso Books.

This is the authoritative account of the development of the students against sweatships movement in the late 1990s.

Peterson, Christopher. 2004. *Taming the Sharks: Towards a Cure for the High Cost Credit Market.* Akron, OH: University of Akron Press.

Here is a book that outlines broader strokes of predatory lending in America that stretch well beyond the fraudulant mortgage practices addressed by ACORN as reported in this chapter. Disappointingly, the book seeks to find a compromise with the "sharks" that would "protect the working poor borrower while preserving economic competition." This is typical thinking, but wrong. The book should seek solutions to protect the working poor "against" economic competition—which by the author's own admission—has sought through history to exploit the poor through predatory lending practices.

Ritzer, George. 2004. *The McDonaldization of Society.* Thousand Oaks, CA: Pine Forge Press.

The strength of this book is the platform it provides for thinking about the impacts of current large-scale corporate business practices from the viewpoint of citizens rather than managers. The book provokes much thought about the impacts and meaning of companies like Wal-Mart, McDonalds, and Home Depot on the community and individual lives of people throughout the world.

CHAPTER 5

The Next Generation: Social Movements Promoting Social Justice in a Globalizing World

This chapter is about bottom-up movements that are in their infancy. They are not strictly U.S. social movements. Instead, they are movements with a more international focus, precisely because they are emerging in response to problems of social justice tendered by the relentless expansion of global economic activity in the world today. They are the next generation of social movements and are already having an impact.

In the first reading, Brian Halwell reports on "The Rise of Food Democracy." Just one of the consequences of rampant economic globalization in the last fifteen years is that small farmers producing products for local food markets are in rapid decline. Not only in the United States, but also all over the world, small farms are being replaced or pressed into the service of large-scale agribusiness operations concerned with building a worldwide food system that delivers any food, any time, anywhere to consumers that pay premium prices. Today's typical supermarket, as Halwell notes, "contains no fewer that 30,000 items, about half of them produced by ten multinational food and beverage companies, with 117 men and 21 women forming the boards of directors of those companies." From Nebraska to Norway and from Egypt to Zimbabwe, Halwell shows how small farmers are responding to reclaim the "sovereignty" of small producers and local markets, with some notable effects at the level of the World Trade Organization and some of the world's largest food companies.

In "Not a Drop to Drink," Kelly Hearn takes up another consequence of globalization—the privatization of public utility services such as water and electricity. Hearn's article focuses on a bottom-up movement that began in Bolivia in 2000 after the Bolivian government, under pressure from the World Bank, privatized local water systems and awarded contracts for water management to international companies like California's Bechtel Corporation and France's Suez Company. The lessons of the Bolivian movements, according to Hearn, are spreading across South America. And there are parallels in the United States, where the deregulation of utilities has led to corporate scandals like

Enron, roving electrical-grid blackouts, and, in response, the formation of a network of hundreds of bottom-up Citizen's Utility Boards (or CUBS).

The third article does not represent a bottom-up social movement. Instead, it illustrates the effects at more elite levels of bottom-up movements like the Bolivian peasant uprising over water services or the small farmers' struggle for food democracy against global agribusiness. Because of these movements—centered at local levels around the world—splits are emerging among national elites at the lofty level of the World Trade Organization (WTO). The WTO is an international forum where leaders from most world nations meet on a scheduled basis to negotiate the international trade agreements that frame the rules for expanding global economic trade (globalization). Notoriously, the rules made at the WTO favor the interests of large-scale multinational corporations based in the United States, Britain, France, Germany, Japan, and the like. But as Martin Khor reports in "Relatively Weak Nations Fight the Policies of the World Trade Organization," leaders from nations in Asia, Africa, and Latin America are forming coalitions to resist the dominant position of developed countries and their corporations in the making of global trade rules. Despite the fact that Americans generally view the elites of developing (or third world) countries as being corrupt and dictatorial, it seems that they are taking a stand for some protection of their people's public services and small farmers from the interests of global business enterprises based in the U.S. and other developed countries. Can Americans say the same thing about the U.S. government's effort to protect their interests against our own global business corporations?

Finally, the last article in this chapter is selected to create more familiarity with an ideology that flames the nascent bottom-up social movements of the globalizing world. As noted in the introduction to this text, "ideology is the key to a movement's success" because it "provides the goal and the rationale for action" and "binds diverse members together in a common cause." To most Americans, and indeed to most residents of the developed world, people in less developed countries do not share our high standard of living because they lag behind us in technological, economic, political, and social development. But Vandana Shiva, a charismatic social movement leader from India, gives a different view (or ideology). She sees the poverty of the third world as a social injustice, a "result of dispossession and deprivation." In these days of the war on terror, it is hard for Americans to understand that anti-American sentiments and movements can stem from anything other than "radical Islamist ideologies." But Shiva's view is much more widespread, and ideologies like it are much more galvanizing for anti-globalization movements in the twenty-first century.

Global economic expansion has drawn new lines for progressive social movements in these times. The new generation of movements will play out to advance equality, democracy, and social justice not only within the nation, but also on a global stage.

The Rise of Food Democracy

BRIAN HALWELL

The National Touring Association, one of the largest lobbying groups in Norway, representing walkers, hikers and campers, recently joined forces with the nation's one and only celebrity chef to develop a line of foods made from indigenous ingredients to stock the country's network of camping huts. For instance, someone staying in a mountain cottage in Jotunheimen National Park would dine on cured reindeer heart, sour cream porridge and small potatoes grown only in those mountain valleys. Sekem, Egypt's largest organic food producer, has developed a line of breads, dried fruits, herbs, sauces and other items made entirely from ingredients grown in the country. The brand is recognized by 70 per cent of Egyptians, and sales have doubled each of the last five years. In Zimbabwe, six women realized that their husbands, who are peanut farmers, were literally getting paid peanuts for their crop while they bought pricey imported peanut butter. These women decided to invest in a grinder and are now producing a popular line of peanut butter from local nuts that sells for 15 per cent less than mainstream brands. In Nebraska, in the United States, a group of local farmers got together and opened a farmers grocery that stocks only foods raised in that State. They found suppliers of bacon and baked beans, sour cream and sauerkraut, and virtually all major grocery items, all from Nebraska.

What ties together these disparate enterprises from around the world? At a time when our food often travels farther than ever before, they are all evidence of "food democracy" erupting from an imperialistic food landscape. At first blush, food democracy may seem a little grandiose—a strange combination of words. But if you doubt the existence of power relations in the realm of food, consider a point made by Frances and Anna Lappé in their book *Hope's Edge* (see UN Chronicle, Issue 3, 2001). The typical supermarket contains no fewer than 30,000 items, about half of them produced by ten multinational food and beverage companies, with 117 men and 21 women forming the boards of directors of

Source: "The Rise of Food Democracy" by Brian Halwell, *UN Chronicle Online Edition*, Vol. XLII, #1, January 2005.

those companies. In other words, although the plethora of products you see at a typical supermarket gives the appearance of abundant choice, much of the variety is more a matter of branding than of true agricultural variety and, rather than coming from thousands of farmers producing different local varieties, they have been globally standardized and selected for maximum profit by just a few powerful executives. Food from far-flung places has become the norm in much of the United States and the rest of the world. The value of international trade in food has tripled since 1961, while the tonnage of food shipped between countries has grown fourfold during a time when populations only doubled. For example, apples in Des Moines supermarkets come from China, even though there are apple orchards in Iowa; potatoes in Lima's supermarkets come from the United States, even though Peru boasts more varieties of potato than any other country.

The long-distance food system offers unprecedented and unparalleled choice to paying consumers—any food, any time, anywhere. At the same time, this astounding choice is laden with contradictions. Ecologist and writer Gary Nabhan wonders "what culinary melodies are being drowned out by the noise of that transnational vending machine," which often runs roughshod over local cuisines, varieties and agriculture. The choice offered by the global vending machine is often illusory, defined by infinite flavouring, packaging and market-ing reformulations of largely the same raw ingredients (consider the hundreds of available breakfast cereals). The taste of products that are always available but usually out of season often leaves something to be desired.

Long-distance travel requires more packaging, refrigeration and fuel, and generates huge amounts of waste and pollution. Instead of dealing directly with their neighbours, farmers sell into a remote and complex food chain of which they are a tiny part and are paid accordingly. A whole constellation of relation-ships within the food shed—between neighbours, between farmers and local processors, between farmers and consumers—is lost in the process. Farmers producing for export often find themselves hungry as they sacrifice the output of their land to feed foreign mouths, while poor urbanites in both the First and Third Worlds find themselves living in neighbourhoods unable to attract most supermarkets and other food shops, and thus without healthy food choices. Products enduring long-distance transport and long-term storage depend on preservatives and additives and encounter all sorts of opportunities for contam-ination on their journey from farm to plate. The supposed efficiencies of the long-distance chain leave many people malnourished and underserved at both ends of the chain.

The changing nature of our food in many ways signals what the changing global economic structure means for the environment, our health and the tenor of our lives. The quality, taste and vitality of foods are profoundly affected by how and where they are produced and how they arrive at our tables. Food touches us so deeply that threats to local food traditions have sometimes provoked strong, even violent, responses. José Bové, the French shepherd who smacked his tractor into a McDonald's restaurant to fight what he called "culinary imperialism," is one of the better-known symbols in a nascent global movement to protect and invigorate local food sheds.

It is a movement to restore rural areas, enrich poor nations, return wholesome foods to cities and reconnect suburbanites with their land by reclaiming lawns, abandoned lots and golf courses to use as local farms, orchards and gardens.

Local food is pushing through the cracks in the long-distance food system: rising fuel and transportation costs; the near extinction of family farms; loss of farmland to spreading suburbs; concerns about the quality and safety of food; and the craving for some closer connection to it. Eating local allows people to reclaim the pleasures of face-to-face interactions around food and the security that comes from knowing what one is eating. It might be the best defense against hazards intentionally or unintentionally introduced in the food supply, including E-coli bacteria, genetically modified foods, pesticide residues and bio-warfare agents. In an era of climate change and water shortages, having farmers nearby might be the best hedge against other unexpected shocks. On a more sensual level, locally grown and in-season food served fresh has a definite taste advantage—one of the reasons this movement has attracted the attention of chefs, food critics and discriminating consumers around the world.

The local alternative also offers huge economic opportunities. A study by the New Economics Foundation in London found that every £10 spent at a local food business is worth £25 for that area, compared with just £14 when the same amount is spent in a supermarket. That is, a pound (or dollar, peso or rupee) spent locally generates nearly twice as much income for the local economy. The farmer buys a drink at the local pub; the pub owner gets a car tune-up at the local mechanic; the mechanic brings a shirt to the local tailor; the tailor buys some bread at the local bakery; the baker buys wheat for bread and fruit for muffins from the local farmer. When these businesses are not locally owned, money leaves the community at every transaction.

This sort of multiplier is perhaps most important in the developing world where the vast majority of people are still employed in agriculture. In West Africa, for example, each $1 of new income for a farmer yields an average increase to other workers in the local economy, ranging from $1.96 in Niger to $2.88 in Burkina Faso. No equivalent local increases occur when people spend money on imported foods. While the idea of complete food self-sufficiency may be impractical for rich and poor nations alike, greater self-sufficiency can buffer them against the whims of international markets. To the extent that food production and distribution are relocated in the community under local ownership, more money will circulate in the local community to generate more jobs and income.

But here's what makes these declarations of food independence, despite their small size, so threatening to the agricultural status quo. They are built around certain distinctions—geographic characteristics—that global trade agreements are trying so hard to eliminate. These agreements, whether the European Union Trade Zone or the North American Free Trade Agreement, depend on erasing borders and geographic distinctions. . . . Multinational food companies that source the cheapest ingredients they can find also depend on erasing these distinctions. . . .

Look around and you can glimpse the change worldwide. Farmers in Hawaii are uprooting their pineapple plantations to sow vegetables in hopes of replacing the imported salads at resorts and hotels. School districts throughout Italy have launched an impressive effort to make sure cafeterias are serving a Mediterranean diet by contracting with nearby farmers. At the rarefied levels of the World Trade Organization, officials are beginning to make room for nations to feed themselves, realizing that this might be the best hope for poor nations that cannot afford to import their sustenance. Even some of the world's biggest food companies are starting to embrace these values, a reality that raises some unsettling questions and awesome opportunities for local food advocates. Recently, officials at both Sysco—the world's largest food-service provider—and Kaiser Permanente—the largest health care provider in the United States—declared their dependence on small local farmers for certain products they cannot get anywhere else. These changes will unfold in a million different ways, but the general path will look familiar. Farmers will plant a greater diversity of crops. Less will be shipped as bulk commodity and more will be packaged, canned and prepared to be sold nearby. Small food businesses will emerge to do this work, Governments will encourage new businesses, and shoppers seeking pleasure and reassurance will eat deliberately and inquire about the origins of their food. Communities world-wide all possess the capacity to regain this control and this makes the simple idea of eating local so powerful. These communities have a choice, and they are choosing instead to eat here.

Not a Drop to Drink: Bolivians Protest Policies of the World Bank

KELLY HEARN

In El Alto, Bolivia, a populist drumbeat is being heard—and it's about water. Protesters say a foreign-owned company contracted to manage the city's water system has failed to get enough of it to El Alto's poor. When protesters shut down a major road, Bolivia's president, Carlos Mesa, axed the state contract with the company, which is part-owned by the gigantic French water corporation Suez.

It's not the first time Bolivian protesters have sent a huge multinational firm packing. In 1997, the World Bank forced Bolivia to privatize its water system as a loan contingent. In 2000, residents of the city Cochabamba took to the streets when connection fees rose steeply after a subsidiary of California-based construction giant Bechtel took over. The Bolivian government violently suppressed the protests, and the events were documented and spread across the Internet by Jim Shultz, founder of the Democracy Project, a Bolivian-based watchdog group.

In the end, Bechtel pulled out and sued the Bolivian government for $25 million under a bilateral investment treaty. The case is now pending. Water privatization has hit bumps in Argentina, too, where President Nestor Kirchner has been sparring with Aguas Argentinas, also a subsidiary of Suez, over claims that the company has not lived up to its infrastructure investment promises. As global freshwater shortages loom, water has become a political pulse point in Latin America, which in recent years has increasingly backed away from the more conservative policies of the 1990s and elected left-leaning governments.

The World Bank estimates that 76 million of the 510 million people in the Caribbean and Latin America do not have access to safe drinking water. Bank officials embrace privatization as a panacea, and multinational corporations are

Source: Reprinted with permission from Kelly Hearn, "Not a Drop to Drink," *The American Prospect Online*: February 25, 2005. The American Prospect, 11 Beacon Street, Suite 1120, Boston, MA 02108. All rights reserved.

happy to get closer to Latin America's vast water supply (when global water shortages really hit, it's nice to be a supplier of last resort).

Here in South America, shoddy delivery and treatment systems, poor oversight, and wasteful cultures of use present their own problems for water. But the great sucking noise will come from trade law, from developing countries signing their water resources over to private companies via deals like the North American Free Trade Agreement (NAFTA) and the Central American Free Trade Agreement (CAFTA), deals that treat water as "goods" and "investments."

The International Forum on Globalization, based in San Francisco, has mapped how noxious provisions from NAFTA, now incorporated into CAFTA, will favor multinational corporations and spell disaster for developing countries.

Consider NAFTA's Chapter 11, the investor-state provision. Locked into CAFTA and favored for inclusion in the Free Trade Area of the Americas (FTAA), the provision lets corporations (investors) sue governments (states) if they feel they have lost out on economic opportunity.

Translation: If any country, state, or province lets only domestic companies export water, corporations in the other signatory countries could sue for financial compensation for "discrimination." And if a government attempted to ban bulk water exports, says Antonia Juhasz, an International Forum on Globalization analyst, the very act would automatically turn water into a tradable commodity, which in turn would trigger the CAFTA or, if it's resuscitated, the FTAA.

Under such a scheme, a lot of Bechtels could sue a lot of Bolivias for money that might otherwise be spent on lifting people from poverty.

Juhasz, in an IFG study, says other trade provisions favored by the U.S. right could spell problems for water-rich developing nations that sign up for regional trade agreements: The idea of "proportional sharing," embedded in NAFTA's article 315, prohibits signatories from restricting resource exports, cutting off a country's ability to curtail water exports. Another is a WTO principle that any new laws, including environmental laws, must be "least trade restrictive," a provision the IFG report says has been the death of many environmental laws. These are concepts that vastly expand the rights of multinational investors trying to get close to Latin America's water systems and supplies. The legalisms may be lost on most Latin Americans, but the greed behind them certainly is not. Judging from their presence on the Internet, the Cochabamba protests seem, like Kent State or Tiananmen Square, to symbolize greater struggles. More than a rejection of water privatization and commodification, they are an indictment of aggressive, U.S.-backed trade policies, of insatiable First World greed, of the corporate march across civil society.

The Economist, citing World Bank statistics, recently reported that privatization in the 1990s expanded the access that Latin Americans have to water by 40 percent to 70 percent. But observers suggest that lower-tech options could come before widespread corporate-favoring privatization contracts. Activists such as Canadian Maude Barlow has suggested radical shifts in watershed management and production, infrastructure repairs, reclamation of outdated water systems, and drip irrigation as opposed to flood irrigation.

Here in South America, the lessons are getting clearer by the protest; the world would do well to study the lessons of Cochabamba and El Alto. Global water shortages, corporate creep, and devastating trade agreements are bringing us fast to a place where, as one water company reportedly described it, water has gone from an endless commodity taken for granted to "a rationed necessity that may be taken by force."

Relatively Weak Nations Fight the Policies of the World Trade Organization

MARTIN KHOR

At a meeting on services at the World Trade Organisation on 28–29 September, developing countries fought back against a proposal by the rich nations to open up their services markets through a new method. Among the countries protesting the moves were Malaysia and several other ASEAN countries. Developing countries have fought back against plans by the rich countries to open up their services markets.

Many groupings of the South, including most ASEAN countries, the Africa Group, the Caribbean countries and many Latin American countries led by Brazil, spoke up strongly against the developed countries' proposals to change the rules in the WTO to accelerate the liberalisation of services in developing countries. In the proposals, developing countries would no longer be able to liberalise at their own pace and in their own chosen sectors, but would have to commit to open up a certain number of key sectors out of a list to be agreed on.

The meeting of the WTO's Services Council was a battleground last week between developed countries (led by the European Union and Japan) and most developing countries over the pace of liberalisation and the policy choices that developing countries will have in future. At stake is the future of local enterprises in areas such as banking, insurance and other financial sub-sectors, telecommunications and other utilities, distribution, and professional services.

Up to now, countries are allowed to choose whether to open up to competition from foreign firms and to what extent in the various sectors, under the General Agreement on Trade in Services (GATS). This is known as the positive-list approach where liberalisation is committed only in sectors inscribed by a country in its services schedules in the WTO. Other countries can request that a particular WTO members open up in more areas, but it is up to that member to

Source: "South Fights Back on Services at WTO" by Martin Khor, *Trends, Third World Network*, October 3, 2005. Reprinted with permission of Third World Network.

respond in the way it wants through offers made in the WTO. This is known as the request-offer method of negotiations.

The rich nations' plans to change this through a multilateral benchmarking approach (where developing countries have to open up in for example six out of ten selected sectors) came under heavy fire at last week's meeting. Some major ASEAN countries were among the most vocal critics. A joint statement by Brunei, Indonesia, Malaysia, the Philippines and Thailand was presented by Philippines Ambassador, Manuel Teehankee. They said the request and offer method should remain the main method of negotiations. "Like many other members, we are still not clear how this will not in effect eventually replace the bilateral request-offer process or reduce it to a mere monitoring process," they said. The proposals also may not adequately cover the developmental dimensions of flexibility for developing countries.

Room for policy maneuver is very crucial, said the ASEAN countries, especially since countries are unable to change their liberalization commitments once they are made, unless they are willing to pay compensation which can be highly punitive. Each member has scheduled its own limitations in sectors, and is allowed to gradually liberalise at its own pace, which takes place when it corresponds to domestic policies. Services liberalisation should also be accompanied by sound macroeconomic management and appropriate regulation and supervision.

"Our authorities continue to carefully consider the pace and sequencing of further liberalisation in sectors together with a comprehensive review of our existing regulatory regime to secure the soundness of our services sectors, especially sensitive systems such as financial services and telecoms." The countries said they are concerned that the proposed approaches may undermine such GATS flexibilities. "A member may be caught in situations where it has no choice but to undertake commitments prematurely to fulfill the targets. This may undermine the principle of progressive liberalisation."

The five ASEAN countries added that the "scoring approach" (a proposal to give scores to countries, with high scores to those that have liberalized more) could send a wrong message. It does not help increase the comparability of schedules but generalises Members' commitments into a simplified value. "The scoring approach will transgress negotiations into viewing services negotiations akin to goods negotiations where one plus one is equal to two," they said. A fair and accurate method to translate commitments into indices is lacking. "It is dangerous to request for an agreement on the desirability of complementary approaches before the design is fully fleshed out. It is comparable to asking for a blank cheque."

The African Group, represented by Egypt, said that establishing any targets would reduce the flexibility inherent in the GATS. Though the proposals claim to be complementary to the request-offer approach, they in fact seek to replace it. The least developed countries said they face structural weaknesses in their local service sectors which would be compounded by the proposals which they therefore rejected.

Several Caribbean countries, represented by Jamaica, rejected the proposals, saying that these undermine the flexibility, and "policy space" allowed by the GATS. Brazil also attacked the proposals for not respecting the structure of the services agreement and the flexibilities given to developing countries. The proposals would also burden mainly the developing countries, while the rich countries would get off free because they had liberalised more of their services before and thus did not have to do more.

The severe criticisms by developing countries have put the developed countries on the defensive for the time. But they are expected to continue to pile on the pressure on this issue.

How to End Poverty: Making Poverty History and the History of Poverty

VANDANA SHIVA

The cover story of the *Time Magazine* of March 14, 2005 was dedicated to the theme, "How to End Poverty." It was based on an essay by Jeffrey Sacks "The End of Poverty," from his book with the same title. The photos accompanying the essay are homeless children, scavengers in garbage dumps, heroin addicts. These are images of disposable people, people whose lives, resources, livelihoods have been snatched from them by a brutal, unjust, excluding process which generates poverty for the majority and prosperity for a few.

[In a] book entitled *Poverty: The Wealth of the People*, an African writer draws a distinction between poverty as subsistence, and misery as deprivation. It is useful to separate a cultural conception of simple, sustainable living as poverty from the material experience of poverty that is a result of dispossession and deprivation. Culturally perceived poverty need not be real material poverty: sustenance economies, which satisfy basic needs through self-provisioning, are not poor in the sense of being deprived. Yet the ideology of development declares them so because they do not participate overwhelmingly in the market economy, and do not consume commodities produced for and distributed through the market even though they might be satisfying those needs through self-provisioning mechanisms. People are perceived as poor if they eat millets (grown by women) rather than commercially produced and distributed processed junk foods sold by global agri-business. They are seen as poor if they live in self-built housing made from ecologically adapted natural material like bamboo and mud rather than in cement houses. They are seen as poor if they wear handmade garments of natural fibre rather than synthetics. Sustenance, as culturally perceived poverty, does not necessarily imply a low physical quality of life. On the contrary, because sustenance economies contribute to the growth

Source: "Making Poverty History and the History of Poverty" by Dr. Vandana Shiva, as appeared on the Navdanya website, www.navdanya.org, 2/7/06.

of nature's economy and the social economy, they ensure a high quality of life measure in terms of right to food and water, sustainability of livelihoods, and robust social and cultural identity and meaning.

Ending poverty requires knowing how poverty is created. However, Jeffrey Sachs views poverty as the original sin. As he declares: A few generations ago, almost everybody was poor. The Industrial Revolution led to new riches, but much of the world was left far behind. This is totally false history of poverty, and cannot be the basis of making poverty history. Jeffrey Sachs has got it wrong. The poor are not those who were left behind, they are the ones who were pushed out and excluded from access to their own wealth and resources. The "poor are not poor because they are lazy or their governments are corrupt". They are poor because their wealth has been appropriated and wealth creating capacity destroyed. The riches accumulated by Europe were based on riches appropriated from Asia, Africa and Latin America. Without the destruction of India's rich textile industry, without the take over of the spice trade, without the genocide of the native American tribes, without Africa's slavery, the industrial revolution would not have led to new riches for Europe or the U.S. It was the violent take over of Third World resources and Third World markets that created wealth in the North—but it simultaneously created poverty in the South.

Two economic myths facilitate a separation between two intimately linked processes: the growth of affluence and the growth of poverty. Firstly, growth is viewed only as growth of capital. What goes unperceived is the destruction in nature and in people's sustenance economy that this growth creates. The two simultaneously created 'externalities' of growth—environmental destruction and poverty creation—are then casually linked, not to the processes of growth, but to each other. Poverty, it is stated, causes environmental destruction. The disease is then offered as a cure: growth will solve the problems of poverty and environmental crisis it has given rise to in the first place. This is the message of Jeffrey Sachs' analysis. The second myth that separates affluence from poverty is the assumption that if you produce what you consume, you do not produce. This is the basis on which the production boundary is drawn for national accounting that measures economic growth.

Both myths contribute to the mystification of growth and consumerism, but they also hide the real processes that create poverty. First, the market economy dominated by capital is not the only economy, development has, however, been based on the growth of the market economy. The invisible costs of development have been the destruction of two other economies: nature's processes and people's survival. The ignorance or neglect of these two vital economies is the reason why development has posed a threat of ecological destruction and a threat to human survival, both of which, however, have remained "hidden negative externalities" of the development process. Instead of being seen as results of exclusion, they are presented as "those left behind." Instead of being viewed as those who suffer the worst burden of unjust growth in the form of poverty, they are falsely presented as those not touched by growth. This false separation of processes that create affluence from those that create poverty is at the core of Jeffrey Sachs analysis. His recipes will therefore aggravate and deepen poverty instead of ending it. Trade and exchange of goods and services have always existed in human societies, but these were subjected to nature's and people's economies. The elevation of the domain of the market and man-made capital to the position of the highest organizing principle for societies has led to the neglect and destruction of the other two organizing principles—ecology and survival—which maintain and sustain life in nature and society.

Modern economies and concepts of development cover only a negligible part of the history of human interaction with nature. For centuries, principles of sustenance have given human societies the material basis of survival by deriving livelihoods directly from nature through self-provisioning mechanisms. Limits in nature have been respected and have guided the limits of human consumption. In most countries of the South large numbers of people continue to derive their sustenance in the survival economy which remains invisible to market-oriented development. All people in all societies depend on nature's economy for survival. When the organizing principle for society's relationship with nature is sustenance, nature exists as a commons. It becomes a resource when profits and accumulation become the organizing principles and create an imperative for the exploitation of resources for the market. Without clean water, fertile soils and crop and plant genetic diversity, human survival is not possible. These commons have been destroyed by economic development, resulting in the creation of a new contradiction between the economy of natural processes and the survival economy, because those people deprived of their traditional land and means of survival by development are forced to survive on an increasingly eroded nature.

People do not die for lack of incomes. They die for lack of access to resources. Here too Jeffrey Sacks is wrong when he says, "In a world of plenty, 1 billion people are so poor, their lives are in danger". The indigenous people in the Amazon, the mountain communities in the Himalaya, peasants whose land has not been appropriated and whose water and biodiversity has not been destroyed by debt creating industrial agriculture are ecologically rich, even though they do not earn a dollar a day. On the other hand, even at five dollars a day, people are poor if they have to buy their basic needs at high prices. Indian peasants who have been made poor and pushed into debt over the past decade to create markets for costly seeds and agrichemicals through economic globalisation are ending their lives in thousands. When seeds are patented and peasants will pay $1 trillion in royalties, they will be $1 trillion poorer. Patents on medicines increase costs of AIDS drugs from $200 to $20,000, and cancer drugs from $2,400 to $36,000 for a year's treatment. When water is privatized, and global corporations make $1 trillion from commodification of water, the poor are poorer by $1 trillion.

The movements against economic globalisation and maldevelopment are movements to end poverty by ending the exclusions, injustices and ecological non-sustainability that are the root causes of poverty. The $50 billion of "aid" North to South is a tenth of $500 billion flow South to North as interest payments and other unjust mechanisms in the global economy imposed by World Bank, IMF. With privatization of essential services and an unfair globalisation imposed through WTO, the poor are being made poorer. Indian peasants are loosing $26 billion annually just in falling farm prices because of dumping and trade liberalization. Unfair, unjust globalisation, is leading to corporate take over of food and water. More than $5 trillion will be transferred from poor people to rich countries just for food and water. The poor are financing the rich. If we are serious about ending poverty, we have to be serious about ending the unjust and violent systems for wealth creation which create poverty by robbing the poor of their resources, livelihoods and incomes.

Jeffrey Sachs deliberately ignores this "taking," and only addresses "giving," which is a mere 0.1% of the "taking" by the North. Ending poverty is more a matter of taking less than giving an insignificant amount more. Making poverty history needs getting the history of poverty right. And Sachs has got it completely wrong.

_____ ADDITIONAL READINGS _____

Cavanagh, John, and Jerry Mander (eds.). 2004. *Alternatives to Economic Globalization.* San Francisco: Berrett-Koehler.

The World Trade Organization's (WTO) General Agreement on Trade in Services (GATS) is ultimately the reason for the water resource disputes in Bolivia and Latin America. This book reveals other problems with GATS (and other WTO agreements), and proposes an alternative approach.

Halwell, Brian. 2004. *Eat Here.* New York: W.W. Norton.

Halwell gives the expanded story of the food democracy movement.

Lappéé, Frances Moore, and Anna Lappéé. 2002. *Hope's Edge: The Next Diet for a Small Planet.* New York: Tarcher/Putnam.

This book tells how the global food chain is becoming concentrated into the hands of few global agribusiness corporations.

Nordstom, Carolyn. 2004. *Shadows of War.* Berkeley: University of California Press.

The nations of the global North and South are not on the same page when it comes to globalization. Nordstrom explains how this can lead to more war than we care to think about.

CHAPTER 6

Involvement in Social Movements: The Importance of Citizen Activism

This section hopes to energize you to act. Bottom-up social movements, as we have shown in the previous readings, are essential to democratic results in favor of ordinary people. In these times when power is left to its own devices, it will seek its own designs. Powerful people continue to design policies and structure social relations in ways that favor corporations, favor the upper classes, and strip the dignity of powerless peoples across the world. In history, ordinary people have stood up to create quakes of change. In both modest and brash ways they have taken part in dissent, and made a difference.

In this chapter we honor some of the people who dissented from power. The chapter begins with an account of Cindy Sheehan, a woman who spoke against war in Iraq in the face of immense pro-war sentiment. In plain-spoken words, she spurred the peace movement in America, suffering arrests, heavy-handed police tactics, and insufferable public criticism by pro-war advocates. At this writing no one knows exactly how Cindy Sheehan's cause may affect America and world. But one thing is sure—she is a voice of democracy from the bottom up.

In the second example we focus on another strident dissident, José Bové, the French farm activist who now leads the peasant agricultural movement called Via Compesina. Bové has developed a career of challenging actions such as destroying corporate property and leading massive public protests in today's emerging worldwide anti-globalization movement. He has paid time for it in jail, but his dissenting views are weighty and passionate. He commands an audience for his views, even in elite U.S. educational institutions, such as in the interview reported here from Yale University in 2005.

There are also behind-the-scenes workers in social movements. Such people are usually neither famous nor notorious. Seldom do they grab the headlines, but frequently they are the backbone and grit of progressive movements. The third article is the story of Charlie Kernaghan, the man whom author Charles Bowden tabs as "Keeper of the Fire" in the still growing movement of student activism against sweatshop labor.

Individuals can take different roles in progressive social movements. People work into social activism differently, each contributing to the advance of democracy, social justice, freedom, and equality in crucial ways. Indeed, the contributions of activists are as important, perhaps even more important, as those of official leaders whose actions the activists contest and hold in check. And just as leaders show certain traits and attitudes in common, so too do activists. In the final article for this volume, philosopher Paul Loeb elaborates the personal traits and convictions that feed social action from the bottom up. They are compassionate traits, and noble ones that embrace humanity.

Cindy Sheehan and the Peace Movement

SARAH FERGUSON

It's not easy being a professional peace mom—especially when everyone wants a piece of you. "I've been staying in a different place every night," says Cindy Sheehan, the 48-year-old California housewife who galvanized the anti-war movement and starred in the march against the Iraq war on Saturday in Washington, D.C.

Since she left her now famous Camp Casey—named for the 24-year-old son she lost in Iraq—outside President Bush's ranch in Crawford, Texas, four weeks ago, Sheehan has been barnstorming the country, touring in a caravan of rented RVs and cars with some three dozen other military families and Vietnam and Iraq war vets. She and her fellow activists have been prowling the halls of Congress, insisting on face time with legislators. On Monday, Sheehan and several other parents of fallen soldiers were among some 370 activists arrested in a mass civil disobedience on the sidewalk outside the White House.

While right-wing critics like Rush Limbaugh like to suggest she's being bankrolled by Move On, Michael Moore, and other elements of the "limousine left," Sheehan's crusade is still very much a grassroots affair. When she and the rest of the Bring Them Home Now tour hit Washington this week to challenge Bush to meet with them and put the heat on Congress for funding the war, they crashed on couches and slept on bunkbeds at an international youth hostel.

That kind of dogged authenticity is the root of Sheehan's power. At Saturday's massive anti-war demonstration, she electrified the crowds with her plea not to let any more moms suffer the agony of losing a child in a war she says is unwinnable and "founded on lies." "We are here today because we don't want to see any more kids come home in coffins," she told the tens of thousands massed before her at the Ellipse. "How many more of other people's children are you willing to sacrifice for the lies?" she demanded, turning her anger toward Congress. "Shame on you for giving [Bush] the authority to invade Iraq."

It's a potent message, and one even hawkish supporters of the war like Senator Hillary Clinton are being forced to acknowledge. Not wanting to fall into the trap of looking callous for refusing a grieving mom, Clinton, Senate Minority leader

Source: "Cindy Sheehan's Big Week in Washington" by Sarah Ferguson, *Village Voice*, September 26, 2005.

Harry Reid, and even the chief of staff of Senate Majority leader Bill Frist agreed to sit down with the military families and Iraq war veterans who trooped through the Capitol all week. On Monday, Sheehan met with Indiana Democrat Dick Lugar, chair of the Senate Foreign Relations Committee—part of a grassroots lobbying push that drew 700 antiwar campaigners to the Hill. Republican senator John McCain is scheduled for a meeting on Tuesday.

For extra motivation, the pols can turn to the polls. A record two thirds of the American public now disapproves of Bush's handling of the war in Iraq, and 52 percent think we should get out "as soon as possible." That's in contrast to an ABC News/Washington Post poll taken two months ago, when 58 percent of those asked said they supported keeping troops in Iraq "until civil order is restored, even if that means continued U.S. military casualties."

Saturday's march, estimated by police at something more than 100,000 people and by organizers at around 300,000, marked a revival of protest on a scale not seen since the start of the U.S. invasion in 2003. More significant than the size of the march was its tone. In contrast to the almost giddy Bush-bashing of previous demos, there was a sense of somber urgency brought by the presence of hundreds of military families and alienated Iraq war vets. Their voices have given the movement a new center of gravity.

"Just like Rosa Parks, Cindy Sheehan has triggered a public policy debate that's bigger than her as a personality," Reverend Jesse Jackson said backstage. "She's unleashed a dynamic that is calling into question the basis of this war."

"You can be against the war and win re-election now. You can be against the war and get elected," Jackson continued. "We have Republicans who are starting to turn on Bush. That was not true a year ago, before Cindy Sheehan and before Katrina."

And that's also why the right is doing its best to derail the Cindy bandwagon, casting her as an anti-American, "professional griever." Beyond dredging for dirt in her personal life, Republican operatives are now trotting out their own pro-military moms in an effort to blunt Sheehan's message. They launched a "You Don't Speak for Me, Cindy" cross-country bus tour, which arrived in Washington on Sunday.

Their rally drew only several hundred supporters to the Washington Mall, where they held up signs like "Freedom Isn't Free" and "Saddam Is a WMD" as they listened to speakers like Watergate thief-turned-radio-pundit G. Gordon Liddy, who accused Sheehan of "whoring the good name of her son" and carrying out a "left-wing socialist agenda."

Also speaking out was Temple, Texas, native Gary Qualls, whose 20-year-old son, Lance Cpl. Louis Qualls, was killed in Falluja last year. Qualls brandished a small white cross, pulled from a memorial Sheehan's group had set up in Crawford, with his kid's name painted on it. "This is the very first cross repossessed from Cindy Sheehan's unholy camp!" he declared, his face red with anger. "We need nothing but pure honor and respect for our service members and for our leader George Bush."

Sheehan offers no way out of this political conflict or this war, and it's hard to say what will become of her iconic status now that she's spun into the orbit of the anti-war left, with both national campaigns like Win Without War and every wing-nut wannabe seeking to glom on to her cause. Monday's civil disobedience ran the gamut of Code Pinkers and Naderites, anarch-kids and feminist boob-flashers, along with some guys roaming around in prison garb, with Abu Ghraib hoods over their heads.

"The whole world is watching," chanted the crowd of supporters as Sheehan took the first bust, blowing a kiss to her followers when the cops loaded her into a van before a scrum of media surging to capture the shot. "The whole thing is scripted," the anarch-kids chanted back.

For now, Sheehan pledges to keep talking, believing more and more people are listening. "It's hard to tell these stories," she says of the sons and husbands that she and other military families have lost. "But we do it to heal ourselves and to heal this country. We do it because we have been broken, and we don't want anyone else to be broken. We're doing it for the innocent Iraqis in harm's way, and we're doing it for the other families, so they don't have to hear that knock on the door."

José Bové and the Global Peasant Movement

At the Yale Center for the Study of Globalization, José Bové attended a workshop in 2005 with prominent Yale scholars to discuss the status of the global peasant movement and the core issues in his work. The discussion was moderated by Jonathan Schell.

INTRODUCTION BY JONATHAN SCHELL

José Bové is an internationally renowned leader of the movement against neoliberal globalization. He is the leader, and founder of the Peasants Confederation in France (La Confederation Paysanne), which enlarged itself to become the peasants' coordinated confederation for all of Europe. Now it's gone global as the Via Campesina. I understand that your role is mainly as an activist and leader of that group.

He's known around the world, above all, for his activism. . . . Most recently, he joined with Greenpeace to intercept the cargo vessel of the Golden Lion, which was carrying 32 thousand tons of transgenic soya to the French port of Lorient. He has been jailed for these contributions to society four times so far, he says. He is also the author of a recent book which has just come out in France, and I hope it'll come out here soon. It's called *Pour La Désobéissance Civique* (In Defense of Civil Disobedience). So we are very thrilled and honored to have him here at the Yale Center for the Study of Globalization to tell us about what he's been up to.

INTRODUCTION BY JOSÉ BOVÉ

First thing I want to say is that I'm very happy to be here. For more than one year, I knew I would come here to Yale. I'll try to talk in English, but I have quite

Source: "Food Should be Left Off the Free Trade Table" by José Bové on *YaleGlobal Online*, April 6, 2005. Reprinted with permission of YaleGlobal Online, © 2005 Yale Center for the Study of Globalization, www.yaleglobal.yale.edu.

poor English—so if I make too many mistakes, I'll ask for translation. The first thing I can say is that I'm a farmer in southern France in a special area which is called Larzac, which has an altitude of 800 meters. And I work with sheep; I milk sheep. I've milked sheep for 30 years. This is a special place because this was my first struggle. One of my first struggles against the government and the French army wanted to take our land to make a military base. We had been struggling for ten years, ending in 1981; we won, and the French army gave us our land. Since then, we've done a lot of things. It became a laboratory on how we can share our land and how young farmers can come and begin farming there. So this is a quite interesting laboratory.

And so, if we want young farmers to go on with farming, it's not the economic problem that is primary for us. The main issue is with the social movement here. People begin farming because they want to live in that area. It's the social issue which is the most important to them, instead of knowing if they have enough income to live. It is interesting to see the dynamics in the rural area.

Now I'm working with Via Campesina, which is our international movement of farmers all over the world. This movement began in 1993 during the Uruguay Round of GATT negotiations. Of course, we began fighting in 1986 when the GATT negotiation began and they decided to include agriculture. This was really, for us, something completely new. This is not just for us farmers in Europe or the United States, but for all the farmers of the world—something was really changing in 1986.

This was the beginning of the worldwide coalition, and we decided in 1992 to make an international coalition. It is quite young—only 10 years old—but now, about 190 organizations from all over the world are inside Via Campesina. We represent 200 million farmers all over the world: in Asia, South America, North America, Europe, Africa. And we are gathering more and more.

Of course, the first time people heard about us was in Seattle in 1999 for the big demonstration. Since then, Via Campesina has been quite well-known, especially in Rome, where the United Nations FAO [Food and Agricultural Organization] is based. So we are working a lot with them.

Via Campesina's main issue is about globalization—about the fact that we don't believe that free trade is good for agriculture and food all over the world. And that's why we decided to invent a new concept, which is "food sovereignty." It means that each population should be able to eat from its own agriculture. The main issue for the farmers is to feed the population where they live: first of all, their own families, also the local market, and then the national market.

Of course, that doesn't mean that we are against trade; trade is only a small part of agriculture—not the main part. We think that all the negotiations about the WTO since 1995 have lessened the possibility for the farmers to feed their own population. We are fighting very strongly. Since Seattle in 1999, we have said that we must take WTO out of agriculture and food. It makes no sense that agriculture and food are inside these negotiations. That doesn't mean that we are against the fact that we should organize the prices of the world, that we have to see how these markets are going. We believe that the most important thing is to protect local agriculture from dumping imports. So this is really the main issue for us.

In the past 15 years of the movement on globalization and agriculture with the WTO, only 10 percent of world agricultural production is in the open market. We understand that all the big transnational corporations want it now to be 20 or 30 percent, but of course, farmers all over the world are resisting this because it makes no sense for their own population. Over 90 percent of food is produced where people live. So we don't understand—and nobody can explain to us—why we need to have free trade for food; that is going exactly in the wrong direction. So this is roughly our principle fight.

After that, we talk within Via Campesina about agrarian reform, landless people, about what we call peasant agriculture.

We also talk about the problems of seeds—the possibility for farmers to use their own seeds—and also the WTO rules on patents. We are fighting also to have seeds free of patents; that's why we are fighting specially against GMOs. Even if GMO had no ecological problems or health problems, we would also be against GMOs on this specific issue: the fact that farmers can't use their own seeds. So these are some of the examples of the troubles of Via Campesina. This is getting bigger and bigger.

Last week, we were in Sumatra, Indonesia. We had a meeting with all the farmers and fisher unions of all the countries that had been destroyed by the Tsunami. The victims, many of them farmers and fishers, decided what they wanted to do and how they wanted to rebuild their houses, where they live and farm. This is very important because for the first time, Via Campesina showed that people are able to define their own issues in this type of situation. And the first thing they said, very clearly: "We don't want food importation; we have enough in our countries to feed our population. We don't want fishermen to come in from other countries to fish; we have to fish our own fish in our small boats. We don't need tourism." The Thai people were saying this very clearly: "Tourism is killing us."

We have very clear examples of fisherman whose houses had been destroyed by the tsunami. Their houses were destroyed and they were not allowed to come back, but new hotels were built in place of their village. So they were very angry about this. It was very interesting to see that when people get together they were able to find new solutions regarding their livelihood.

QUESTION FROM JONATHAN SCHELL

Perfect summary of what you're up to. Let me begin. Using agriculture as an example. You know, if you're opposed to the neo-liberal system, how big a bite do you think you have to take out of it to make it right? How large of a reform? Does it have to be a whole new system? Does it have to be a fundamental reform, a superficial reform? What do you think?

JOSÉ BOVÉ REPLIES

Well, you asked me before about the term "globalization." The problem is that in French and in English, we don't have the same words. I remember in Seattle, we were talking about corporate globalization. That's very clear to everyone. Who wants that? In France it is more complicated, because we're not just talking about corporate globalization, we're talking about "mondialisation." And this is a positive word. Because we don't know about what kind of globalization we're talking about. Mondialisation could be anything: It could be culture; it could be all kinds of things—positive and negative.

In France, we had to find a new word, and it should be a positive word. And the first time in the newspaper they called it "anti-mondialisation," against mondialisation. So we found a new word, and the Belgian people who came up [with] the word "alter-mondialisation," which means another type of globalization. And when we talk about globalization now in France, it's very clear that it's corporate globalization. But when we talk about alter-mondialisation, it refers to different kind of issues. That's why the symbol of this is what we said at Porto Alegre at the World Social Forum: "Another world is possible."

I think it is very important not to say that only one other kind of globalization is possible, but that for a lot different reasons, we have to make a world with more than one solution. For different populations we have different ways of life, and it's very dangerous to consider everybody in the same way—either good or bad. So I think it is important, first, that there is not only one good way and one bad way. We need to find different kinds of solutions for different kinds of problems.

Second, it is dangerous for us to say that globalization is only economic globalization. And that all the international rules now are made only about this issue. It makes no sense that the international economic institutions—the Bretton Woods institutions—are more important now than the United Nations. This is getting to be a very big problem. The only international institution that can enforce justice is the WTO. Of course, it is not really democracy when you have an institution like the WTO, which is the executive, the legislative, and the judicial. We've learned a lot from Montesquieu in France about the separation of the powers in democracy. The WTO is the exact opposite of that.

We have to have a lot of reflection about this. What are the good institutions? How do they work? How is it possible that only the economic institutions have their own justice and bring sentences against countries, but at the same time, the United Nations is unable to enforce sanctions when there are problems with human rights, environmental problems, labor problems, and so on. This means that now, we must reflect about how these institutions work, which are the most important, how to make new regulations among the international laws, human rights, trade, environment, work, and so on. We have to say very clearly that trade has to be under the human rights, environmental, and so on. It's impossible to simply make rules to open the market and then see what happens after—and say, "We don't care about it. What is most important for us is to open the market. This is going to be the best way for people to live." At this moment this is not true—and mostly for the farmers.

We have more and more problems. The UNFAO reported the number of people dying from hunger as 852 million—it's still a very big problem. More than 60 percent of these people are farmers. This means that the more you open the doors of the countries, the more problems come in. So it's the wrong answer to the problem of hunger. When we talk about the problem of hunger, we have to change the rules and protect the people and the countries—especially the poor countries. I want to emphasize that at this moment, I think that Europe is worse than the United States with globalization. People, in general, think that Europe is not moving in the same direction as the United States; this is not true. During the last negotiation in Cancun, the European Trade Commissioner, Pascal Lemy, was, I think, worse than [US Trade Representative Robert B.] Zoellick regarding opening the markets. This is because in Europe, they want very strongly to open the markets for services. And they want to win this fight for services. And for this, they are willing to do very bad things. The European Union at this moment is very dangerous on these issues.

QUESTION FROM GUSTAV RANIS

You say you're not against trade. I'm trying to understand how far you would take your argument. Where do you draw the line between trade you find acceptable and trade that you find unacceptable? I can see why you are worried about security: In case of war or crisis of some sort, you can't depend on imports, and you want to have some nest-egg to ensure that people can feed themselves. I'm just trying to get a sense of where you would draw the line. I'm sure you don't want everybody to be self-sufficient at the expense of efficiency completely. And what about other things [beside] agriculture?

JOSÉ BOVÉ REPLIES

So maybe first thing, which I think is important to know—generally people don't know this—is the fact that 55 percent of the people working now on the earth are farmers. That means that the main issue in the world is agriculture—more than 55 percent. Most of these people are working only with their hands. You can see that at this moment there are 1.6 billion farmers in the world. And with all these, there are only 28 million tractors in the whole world. And of course this means that we have different kinds of issues with different kinds of agriculture.

Very special countries can destroy all this. This is dangerous because it's not only political problems between the countries; it's also a very big social problem inside the countries. For example, this is the main problem with China—we know very clearly, and Chinese economists say this—between 300 and 400 million farmers are going to be put out of their farms in China. The second problem is we don't know what they are going to do. There is not going to be enough work in the factories because the factories are not as they were 50 years ago, so there is going to be a lot of unemployment. What are these people going to do and where are they going to go? And so on. This is really a very important problem.

When we say that we need food sovereignty, it of course does not mean that all the countries have to be able to grow all they need for their own people. But we are talking about groups of countries. . . . Very small countries may sometimes be difficult, so several countries can work together. The problem is to be able to feed their population or to decide at what level they want to protect their own agriculture. Some countries have to import because it's impossible for them to grow their agriculture. So the countries should be able to decide themselves at what level they want to protect their agriculture.

And right now, it's not possible. We saw it in Asia and Africa, with the WTO rules, which impose importing at least 4 percent of their production. Even if they have enough, they have to open their doors to productions from outside—and we know that caused a lot of problems in a lot of countries, in Asia, for rice, for example. And this is still going on there. That's why they are having big fights in South Korea right now. That's why Indonesia is fighting after the Tsunami, saying, "We don't want to open our doors to food coming from outside. We have enough rice, and if we open our doors, all the prices will go down." So it's very important that countries or groups of countries be able to protect themselves from dumping. . . .

MORE QUESTIONS FROM GUSTAV RANIS

The second part of my question is where you draw the line? Do you want the same thing for textiles, for example, or for steel—where do you draw the line?

JOSÉ BOVÉ REPLIES

When I say agriculture, the main issue is that most of the people on earth are working with agriculture. The second problem about textile or other industries: Something quite new is happening—competition. A lot of factories in Europe and United States delocalize their production in southern countries only to have lower costs of production for labor. This doesn't change a lot about what comes back to the southern countries, because most of this money goes back to the big transnational corporations.

If we look at all the money which is going all over the earth with globalization, we see that more than two-thirds of this money goes only to the transnational corporations—or it's money from one transnational to another one. Only one-third is really going to the people or to the countries. This is a really big problem.

For the first time, we see this also with agriculture: delocalization, for example, of chicken production from France to Brazil—with the same company. It's a better situation for them because soya is cheaper; the workers are cheaper. And when they send the chicken back to Europe, Brazil doesn't have the same WTO conditions as France. So it's better for them. With this kind of delocalization, the company is growing more and more.

I don't think that we have to fight against delocalization. But what kind of rules should we have to give the profit to the people? For the moment, there is no benefit for the workers. . . .

QUESTION FROM LAURA WEXLER

You spoke about sufficiency in terms of the farmer, I'm interested in what your organization thinks about the migrant laborer, the workers—who are not farmers—who work on the farms. What do you think about their situation as you go forth in this campaign?

JOSÉ BOVÉ REPLIES

Of course, our organization works also with the workers that work on the big enterprises, especially for sugar and fruit. They work with us; we have the same problem also in Europe, because we see that most times in this kind of enterprise there are more and more migrants involved—and illegal migrants. And of course, their situation is getting worse and worse. And they have a lot of problems in the south of Europe, in Spain, for example, which is one [of] the main places for production of vegetables in greenhouses (which are not green houses, they are plastic houses). Thousands and thousands of hectares of them.

This is really one of the biggest problems now. We have this, of course, in South America, Asia—so it's a difficult situation for them. That's why we are trying to work with the United Nations human rights commission to write the rights of the farmers and workers. And we want to impose the rights at the international level to be able to say "These rights exist, so now you have to go along with this." It's very long work. The people in Indonesia were the first to begin to do this.

The second step is agrarian reform: giving land to landless people. Because very often people who are in these work conditions are former farmers or small farmers who have put out of their land by big enterprise. . . .

Charlie Kernaghan, Keeper of the Fire: Student Activism against Sweatshop Labor

CHARLES BOWDEN

He stands off to the right of the stage, all suit and tie, wire-rimmed glasses and neatly trimmed beard. His body leans back, almost bends like a bow, his 6-foot frame taut, the blue eyes focused, the muscles of his face tight. He is about to launch. Charlie Kernaghan explains, "This isn't a lecture. I have nothin' to teach anyone." He's 55 years old, the hair largely gray now, all duded up like a college professor, and he's backed by a huge American flag in this union hall in Ashland, Ohio. He looks out at a night meeting of 60 or 70 men and women who wear baseball caps blazing with American flags or shouting "UAW." Kernaghan slips into the zone, this state where he is an instrument of some other power, and when he hits the zone, well, my God, he becomes in-your-face messages. Charlie's voice half shouts with a strangled quality; the eyes shrink and become intense. The workers are attentive but at first cannot find a handle to grip in the barrage of words. Last year he made 68 speeches, flew 84,000 miles. He's got the speech down pat. He'll hold up a photograph of some Bangladeshi kid who's sewn stuff for Disney and shout, "SHE MAKES 17 CENTS AN HOUR. DO THE MATH."

Technically, he is a part of the National Labor Committee, a letterhead group of four or five in a small warren of rooms loaned by UNITE in New York City. But beneath this facade he is an independent, a man controlled by no backers, free of any union, immune to academic nuance. He is mildly famous in some circles as the man who made Kathie Lee Gifford cry on camera when he revealed that her clothing line, one peddled by Wal-Mart, was made by kids in Third World sweatshops. The kids made pennies an hour; Kathie Lee took home about $9 million a year for loaning out her name. When Kernaghan first saw her face

Source: Anderson Grinberg Literary Management, Inc.: Excerpt from "Keeper of the Fire" by Charles Bowden, from *Mother Jones* magazine (July/August, 2003). Copyright © 2003 by Charles Bowden. Reprinted by permission of Anderson Grinberg Literary Management, Inc.

on a label in Honduras he did not know who she was. Watching television is one of many things he's skipped for about 15 years. But when she denounced him on national television for telling lies about her, he directed the media to a sweatshop making her togs about a mile from her ABC studio.

Tonight, in the union hall, he hits his riffs. Ashland is basic America, unions crashing, factories fleeing, jobs disappearing. About 83 percent of all garments sold in the United States are now made offshore, as are 80 percent of the toys, 90 percent of the sporting goods, 95 percent of the shoes. The people who make these items largely work in sweatshops for pennies an hour. The companies who commission the work, the famous brand names, buffer themselves from employing slaves and children by using brokers to contract out the work. Kernaghan wants to pull the mask off this practice and end it. Everything he does is simply a means to this end.

"We've lost more than 2 million manufacturing jobs in the last two years," Kernaghan announces. "Last year China surpassed the U.S. as the destination of foreign investment, manufacturing is being dismantled, the consumer is being hurt, the economy is stagnant. In the last two years China has created 30 million jobs and the U.S. HAS LOST 2 MILLION."

He starts pulling clothing out of a bag. He holds up a Wal-Mart item and says, "THERE IS BLOOD ON THIS GARMENT," and then rattles on about the Vietnamese women, imported to an American Samoan factory, who made it, the way they were beaten and kept behind wire, fed gruel and sexually used, the wages they were paid. The facts slap the union members in the face; the bodies suddenly tighten and sit up alert on the hard seats. Enslaved women and kids? Making the clothes on my back? He rolls on with the Gap, Disney, Nike, label after label tied to tales of Third World horror. "If you listen to Nike," he snorts, "you'd think they were a religious organization." He holds up a Nike jersey that retails for $140 but is made by women in El Salvador for 29 cents each. Kernaghan presents a Nike memo he salvaged from the local dump, a favorite research site, that breaks the sewing of another garment into 22 steps, each step timed to a ten-thousandth of a second, all totaling 6.6 minutes. He rolls on that wages account for 10 percent of the retail price of a garment made in the U.S., but only one-third of 1 percent of the price of a garment made in the Third World.

"This," he spits out, "is the true face of the global economy. Labor has been erased. . . ." Kernaghan's hands wave; he is possessed. He holds up a huge photo of a 13-year-old girl in Bangladesh: "This is the real face of Wal-Mart. She only had two days off in the last four months. She's never ridden a bicycle. Seven cents an hour."

After an hour he takes a break, then resumes and goes for another hour. After that it takes Kernaghan a half-hour to get out of the hall as people keep button-holing him. He owns them. And he needs a beer. He's not cut out for this stuff, he contends. He had other dreams. Afterward, he heads for a downtown bar,

Bullshooters, a den of boozy young people being assaulted by rustbelt karaoke singers. He is at ease there. He is back home.

Kernaghan was born one of three children in Brooklyn to immigrant parents. His mother a Czech, his father a Scot in the trades. His older brother studied to become a priest; his sister was a manager. Charlie, after an education at a Marianist high school on Long Island and at Loyola University in Chicago, became a perpetual graduate student. His family was devoutly Catholic and his parents also raised 17 foster children. His father kept taking out bank loans to adopt the kids and kept being denied because of the age of himself and his wife.

Charlie tried psychology, then anthropology, at various schools. Inevitably, he'd be sitting in a class, wonder what in the hell he was doing, walk out and hit the road-for Europe, the Middle East. He still has powerful memories of things such as the feel of night by the Dead Sea when the jackals come out. In between bouts of wandering, he'd hole up in a cheap room and read endlessly. In the early '80s, his father, in despair, got him a carpenters' union card and Kernaghan showed up his first day with a hammer borrowed from his mom and totally incompetent. He worked on remodeling Steve Ross' office at Warner Communications. There was one big room where Ross stored his personal stock certificates. There was a black glass-and-marble bathroom with a special magazine rack by the toilet. One day, Charlie had to install a phone in the bathroom, glued it in upside down, and the whole smoked glass wall had to be trashed. He made $47,000 in six months and quit. . . .

He can't speak a foreign language, use a computer, or type. He constantly says he is frightened, terrified, and scared shitless. He'd never given a speech before he got into this thing, he's disorganized, he fucks up, he can't keep track of things, he creates disorder. Charlie Kernaghan constantly ticks off a list of his failings and limits and terrors. He is almost unconscious of this recurring litany because he not only believes it—he feels it. He is the basic unit in how things get done: someone working past his level of confidence, making it up as he goes along, falling through space, spooked but enthralled as the air streams across his face. He can keep going only because of what he always refers to as "the work." And the work can get done only so long as he never defines it or analyzes it or probes around its dark shadows where the cobwebs might brush his face.

The work is clarity and a mystery. He can't be calm—Kernaghan must run each day in an effort to sedate himself. In El Salvador in 1985, he spent three days with peasants in the San Salvador cathedral they occupied, got a crash course in lack of rights for working people, and decided to do something about it. While down there, Kernaghan hooked up with the National Labor Committee (NLC), a group created by the Reverend David Dyson, a Presbyterian minister who'd come out of the labor movement. As the Central American wars wound down and interest in the NLC declined, Kernaghan, now living in New York, kept it afloat. "You don't just throw away connections like that," he reasoned.

He met Barbara Briggs in 1986 when she dropped by the NLC office in New York. She'd just graduated from University of Massachusetts at Amherst and wanted to go to Central America, learn Spanish, and help unions. "One of those goofy college things," Charlie told her. He explained that nobody down there needed more radical tourists—they needed support from people living in the United States. She went anyway, and he'd bump into her on trips he'd make to Central America and they'd go on dates. At the end of 1988, she agreed to come to New York and help him run the NLC. It became functionally a committee of two. . . .

"I'm shy," he says softly. "It is hard for me to network. I had to learn to overcome a lot of stuff. It was torture in the beginning. I had to dress up; I had no clothes. A friend in my building had a suit I'd borrow, a size 42. I'd look like a clown. I was all right sitting down but when I stood up, it was like I was in a bag. I feel better around working people. I don't feel comfortable around professional people—I have no small talk. . . ."

After a spell, he and Barbara are living together and find their rhythm of working from about 8 a.m. until about 10 p.m. every day of the week. He handles the stump speaking; she feels more comfortable sitting on the academic panels that make Charlie uneasy. They are both tireless and seem at ease with their division of labor in the grand project called "the work." His photography ends; he stops reading anything but documents. He falls into what looks like a hole but feels like a life.

The morning after the union talk, Kernaghan addresses a leadership meeting in Ashland, a room full of business types. He is relentless as he flings his facts: Huffy Bicycle Co., Celina, Ohio, $11 an hour plus $6 an hour in benefits, 750 workers, moved to China, now the workers are paid 25 to 35 cents an hour, 66-hour workweek. "Have we ever heard from any of these workers, just once?"

Then comes the drive across Ohio, a corner of Pennsylvania, and east across New York. He keeps spotting deer in the snow, revels in the woods and hills. His family has a broken-down cabin in the Adirondacks that his folks bought decades ago but he hardly ever has time to go there. Kernaghan is constantly on his cell phone with Barbara thrashing out plans, and the man of professed disorder seems very orderly and exact.

In between calls and wildlife sightings, he wanders back through past campaigns, a history of intuitive moves underscored by an almost tactical genius. Kernaghan seems born to make the back pages of the global economy suddenly leap onto front pages.

"I found a way to sublimate a lot of things," he allows. "I'm not very smart, but I focus and the more focused you are the freer you are. I never get tired. It seems incredible that you can have an impact on these big companies. I don't do anything else. You get an incredible amount done. . . ."

He is everywhere, accompanied by donated film crews. He puts out tapes with titles like Zoned for Slavery and they circulate in the tens of thousands, especially on college campuses.

He is against boycotts since they put people out of work who are barely hanging on as it is. He accepts the global economy as a reality, not an option. At first, Kernaghan sought to get companies to agree to codes of conduct that would be monitored by independent human-rights groups. But as time went on, he realized the scale of the labor migration offshore made such a tactic hopeless. Wal-Mart, for example, contracts with 4,400 plants in just one province of China. Then he sensed a window of opportunity for passing federal legislation that would outlaw the import of items made by children or in sweatshops, a kind of federal consumer guarantee that the goods in U.S. stores are pure and clean. He figured the biggest market in the world could impose such a demand if it wished.

And so now, as he drives across New York State and fields phone calls, he is all about building a coalition of lawyers, church people, unions, and students to demand such legislation. He notes bitterly that trademarks such as Mickey Mouse are rigorously protected in the global economy but workers' rights are considered irrelevant. He is determined to change that. He is relaxed and yet always coiled. Once, in an airport, his cell phone failed to function even as he stood surrounded by others cheerfully talking on their cell phones. So he smashed his phone to pieces on the floor.

About 90 students show up at the auditorium of a state college in Oneonta, New York, most gang-pressed by teachers to attend. Kernaghan begins by saying, "This is gonna be relatively painless. I'm not goin' to lecture, I'm just gonna tell some stories." He roars the speech—90 percent of the imported sporting goods, and 80 percent of the toys, and so forth. "All over the world the people making products for us are young people like yourself," he explains. "When your life is taking off, the lives of young people who make things for you are over—they're thrown out on the street about age 30. Nike's game plan is to put the swoosh on your forehead. The greatest nightmare the corporations have is that you wake up. You have the ability to free your brothers and sisters." Then he picks up a Wal-Mart shirt made in American Samoa. ("There's blood on this shirt. . . .") About seven minutes into his talk, the bodies tighten, the eyes suddenly focus, the fidgeting stops. He owns them.

He tends to use both hands. He'll explain corporate greed by holding up his right hand, spreading thumb and forefinger all the way apart like a big pipe wrench, and saying, "Profits." Then he'll hold his left hand, the thumb and forefinger only millimeters apart, and say, "Labor costs." Or he pours an invisible pitcher from his right to his left hand, showing how companies drain the lives out of the workers. He seems totally unaware of these movements; they have no theatrical ease but seem the inescapable expression of the tension rising off his body.

Later, he winds down at an Italian restaurant. On the wall is an autographed photo of James Gandolfini, star of The Sopranos, with the owner. Kernaghan does not know who he is. He digs into his ravioli and pronounces it "delicious."

He drinks a German beer and finds it also "delicious." He is asked just what the hell he means by his constant expression, "the work," and he falls into a pool of silence for a minute or two.

Then he says with almost strangled passion, "It's very much like a fantasy. My family was all-inclusive love. I was set loose like a cannon. That, combined with religion, blew the whole thing to shreds. . . . My parents were disturbed by me, worried about me finding a career. But they sent me off in a direction where I could live for meaning. Life is precious. I fuckin' hate injustice. No one should interpret our lives—we should speak for ourselves."

The next day he's back in New York, plotting a demonstration at an upcoming Disney shareholder meeting. He's got three Mickey Mouse suits lined up and, of course, will keep one eye cocked for the Keepers of the Fire.

And he'll have running through his mind a calculation he once made: At the time, Phil Knight of Nike had a personal fortune of $5 billion. If Knight flew around the world first class, Charlie figured, that would consume only $11,027. If he stayed in a good room at the Waldorf, that would run $400 and even the best breakfast could swallow only $153. If he bought a new Lincoln Continental, that would get rid of $39,660. If he ratcheted up his consumption and flew around the world every day, stayed at the Waldorf and had three fine meals a day, and bought a new Lincoln every week, he'd still be okay for the next 781 years.

"Why does anyone need that kind of money?" Kernaghan asks. And when he asks this question, he looks absolutely baffled.

The Impossible Will Take a Little While

PAUL ROGAT LOEB

A few years ago, I heard Archbishop Desmond Tutu speak at a Los Angeles benefit for a South African project. He'd been fighting prostate cancer, was tired that evening, and had taken a nap before his talk. But when Tutu addressed the audience he became animated, expressing amazement that God had chosen his native country, given its shameful history of racial oppression, to provide the world with an unforgettable lesson in reconciliation and hope. Afterwards, a few other people spoke, then a band from East L.A. took the stage and launched into an irresistibly rhythmic tune. People started dancing. Suddenly I noticed Tutu boogying away in the middle of the crowd. I'd never seen a Nobel Peace Prize winner, still less one with a potentially fatal illness, move with such joy and abandonment. Tutu, I realized, knows how to have a good time. Indeed, it dawned on me that his ability to recognize and embrace life's pleasures helps him face its cruelties and disappointments, be they personal or political.

Few of us will match Tutu's achievements, but we'd do well to learn from someone who spent years challenging apartheid's brutal system of human degradation, yet has remained light-hearted and free of bitterness. What allowed Tutu, Nelson Mandela, and untold numbers of unheralded South Africans to find the vision, strength, and courage to persist until apartheid finally crumbled? How did they manage to choose forgiveness over retribution while bringing to justice the administrators and executioners of that system? What similar strengths of spirit drove those who challenged entrenched racial segregation in the United States, or the dictatorships of Eastern Europe and Latin America? What now enables ordinary citizens to continue working to heal their communities and to strive for a more humane world, despite the perennial obstacles, the frequent setbacks?

We live in a time fraught with uncertainty and risk. From terrorist threats, pre-emptive wars, and high-level corporate crime, to skyrocketing health care costs, mounting national debt, and an economy that appears rigged for the benefit

Source: From *Impossible Will Take a Little While* by Paul Rogat Loeb. Copyright © 2004 by Paul Rogat Loeb. Reprinted by permission of Basic Books, a member of Perseus Books, L.L.C.

of the greedy and ruthless, the world can at times seem overwhelming, beyond our control. I write these words a few months after Europe's hottest summer on record, when a series of heat waves took an estimated 35,000 lives, more than ten times the toll of the attacks in New York City and Washington, D.C., on September 11, 2001. Worldwatch founder, Lester Brown, and other respected experts, drawing on an ever-growing body of sobering scientific research, attribute the deadly weather to global warming. How difficult it is, though, to address such looming realities as weather gone haywire or a faltering economy when the day-to-day demands of job and family require so much of our attention. Merely thinking about them is to flirt with despair.

And no one is immune, not even those whose occupations or interests directly involve helping others or bringing about constructive social change. In recent years, I've traveled throughout the country to deliver lectures. Almost everywhere, I've encountered people who question whether their actions really matter, whether it's worthwhile to continue making the effort. I've heard this refrain from teachers struggling to help their students learn in inner-city classrooms; from nurses and doctors trying to deliver high-quality medical services while navigating bureaucratic HMO mazes; from Republican Chamber of Commerce members attempting to save small rural towns from going under. I've heard it from eighteen-year-old students and eighty-year-old grandmothers. I've heard it particularly from those who marched and spoke out against the 2003 Iraq War—then were dismissed, in the words of a Minnesota student, "as if all of our efforts were worthless."

But as understandable as such moments of doubt and apparent impotence may be, especially in a culture that too often rewards cynicism and mocks idealism, they aren't inevitable. If tackling critical common problems seems a fool's errand, it's only because we're looking at life through too narrow a lens. History shows that the proverbial rock can be rolled, if not to the top of the mountain, then at least to successive plateaus. And, more important, simply pushing the rock in the right direction is cause for celebration. History also shows that even seemingly miraculous advances are in fact the result of many people taking small steps together over a long period of time. For every Tutu, there have been thousands of anonymous men and women who were equally principled, equally resolute. It's the same indomitable spirit expressed in the Billie Holiday lyric and World War II Army Corps of Engineers motto that inspired the title: "The difficult I'll do right now. The impossible will take a little while."

Political and personal hopes are intertwined, of course. What keeps us committed to improving our communities and our country is akin to what gives us the strength to endure the sometimes devastating difficulties of our individual lives. But my primary focus is on what moves us beyond mere personal survival, beyond carving out a comfortable private existence, to broader, more enduring visions that can help us tackle common problems and keep on doing so regardless of the frustrations we may encounter. We can't afford the sentimental view that mere self-improvement, no matter how noble in intention, is enough. Nor can we afford to succumb to fear.

This isn't to say that fear is unfounded. Any clear-eyed view of the world recognizes that grave threats exist. I've already mentioned some of the most troubling: terrorism, war, economic ruin, global warming. To make matters worse, those in power often take advantage of large-scale threats, including those that are exaggerated or entirely manufactured, by exploiting fear and feelings of vulnerability for their own gain. Today, fear so dominates American society that people hesitate to speak out against such exploitation, worried that they may be deemed unpatriotic or simply ignored, marginalized. And how can people who are afraid to voice their beliefs be able to act on those beliefs, a far riskier endeavor? When fear dictates what we say and do, democracy itself is imperiled. The antidote to such paralysis is hope: defiant, resilient, persistent hope, no matter what the odds against us may be. As Jim Wallis, editor of the evangelical social justice magazine *Sojourners*, writes, "Hope is believing in spite of the evidence, then watching the evidence change."

ORIENTATION OF THE HEART

Another way of expressing Wallis's sentiment is that hope is a way of looking at the world—more than that, it's a way of life. Nowhere is this more apparent than in the stories of those who, like Tutu and Mandela, persist under the most dangerous conditions, when simply to imagine aloud the possibility of change is deemed a crime or viewed as a type of madness. Consider Václav Havel, the former Czech president, whose country's experience, he argues, proves that a series of small, seemingly futile moral actions can bring down an empire. When the Czech rock band Plastic People of the Universe was first outlawed and arrested because the authorities said their Zappa-infuenced music was "morbid" and had a "negative social impact," Havel organized a defense committee; that, in turn, evolved into the Charter 77 organization, which set the stage for Czechoslovakia's broader democracy movement. As Havel wrote, three years before the Communist dictatorship fell, "Hope is not prognostication. It is an orientation of the spirit, an orientation of the heart."

How does a person come by such an orientation? The life of Rosa Parks offers a telling clue, provided we look beyond the conventional retellings of her experience, which actually obscure how the power of the human spirit prevails in bleak times. We think, because we've been told again and again, that one day Parks stepped onto a bus in Montgomery, Alabama, and single-handedly and without apparent preparation inaugurated the civil rights movement by refusing to sit in the segregated section. I remember Garrison Keillor, one Martin Luther King Day, saying, "Rosa Parks wasn't an activist. She was just a woman with her groceries who was tired."

Such accounts, however well-meaning, belie a much more complex reality: that Parks had by that time been a civil rights activist for twelve years, was the secretary of the local chapter of the National Association for the Advancement of Colored People (NAACP), and acted not alone but in concert with and on behalf of others. The summer before her arrest, she'd taken a ten-day workshop and met with an older generation of civil rights activists at the Tennessee labor and civil rights center, Highlander Folk School, which is still going strong today. The first NAACP meeting that Parks attended addressed the issue of lynching, an all-American form of terrorism so accepted in respectable circles that gentlemen smoking cigars and ladies in their Sunday best allowed photos to be taken of themselves standing in front of black men being burned and hanged. Out of this bleak legacy and, more important, the years of struggle to overcome it, came the courage and determination of Parks and people like her, the community of like-minded souls I mentioned earlier.

Nothing cripples the will like isolation. By the same token, nothing buoys the spirit and fosters hope like the knowledge that others faced equal or greater challenges in the past and continued on to bequeath us a better world. Even in a seemingly losing cause, one person may unknowingly inspire another, and that person yet a third, who could go on to change the world, or at least a small corner of it. Rosa Parks's husband, Raymond, convinced her to attend her first NAACP meeting, the initial step on a path that brought her to that fateful day on the bus in Montgomery. But who got Raymond Parks involved? And why did that person take the trouble to do so? What experiences shaped their outlook, forged their convictions? The links in any chain of influence are too numerous, too complex to trace. But being aware that such chains exist, that we can choose to join them, and that lasting change doesn't occur in their absence, is one of the primary ways to sustain hope, especially when our actions seem too insignificant to amount to anything.

COMMUNITY OF CONVICTION

I often turn to the following story, a more personal but equally impressive version of the Parks episode, as a reminder of how powerful a community inspired by conviction can be, even though the members of that community may be unknown to each other, or may be living in different places or historical times. In the early 1960s, a friend of mine named Lisa took two of her kids to a Washington, D.C. vigil in front of the White House protesting nuclear testing. The demonstration was small, a hundred women at most. Rain poured down. The women felt frustrated and powerless. A few years later, the movement against testing had grown dramatically; and Lisa attended a major march. Benjamin Spock, the famous baby doctor, spoke. He described how he'd come to take a stand, which because of his stature had already influenced thousands, and would reach far more when he challenged the Vietnam War. Spock talked directly about the issues, then mentioned that when he was in D.C. a few years earlier he saw a small group of women huddled, with their kids, in the rain. It was Lisa's group. "I thought that if those women were out there," he said, "their cause must be really important."

When the unforeseen benefits of our actions are taken into account, any effort may prove more consequential than it seems at first. In 1969, Richard Nixon's envoy, Henry Kissinger, told the North Vietnamese that the president would escalate the Vietnam War, and even use nuclear strikes, unless they capitulated and forced the National Liberation Front in the South to surrender as well. Nixon had military advisers prepare detailed plans, including mission folders with photographs of potential nuclear targets. But two weeks before the president's November 1 deadline, there was a nationwide day of protest, the Moratorium; millions of Americans joined local demonstrations, vigils, church services, petition drives, and other forms of opposition. The next month, more than half a million people marched in Washington. An administration spokesperson announced that Nixon had watched the Washington Redskins football game and that the demonstrators wouldn't affect his policies in the slightest—thereby feeding the frustration of far too many in the peace movement and accelerating the descent of a few into violence. Yet privately, as we now know from Nixon's memoirs, he decided the movement had, in his words, so "polarized" American opinion that he couldn't carry out his threat. Moratorium participants had no idea that their efforts may have helped stop a nuclear attack.

Although we may never know, it's possible that America's recent peace movement similarly helped make further wars against such countries as Iran and Syria less likely, even before our troops became mired in the shooting gallery of the Iraqi occupation. Whatever one thinks of the invasion of Iraq, and certainly there were people of goodwill on both sides of the debate, several million ordinary Americans marched and spoke out in attempts to prevent it—the largest such protest in at least two decades, and, for many, their first public stand, or their first in years. It wasn't easy to voice opposition, because the Bush administration overtly linked dissent with being an "ally of terrorism." Yet people did, in every community in the country, joined by the biggest global peace demonstrations in history. This movement may have inspired the next Rosa Parks, Benjamin Spock, or Susan B. Anthony. It certainly marked the first steps for innumerable individuals who may be more emboldened in the future, possibly becoming the unsung heroes who ultimately create any change.

THIS GORGEOUS WORLD

But that's true only if the newly engaged don't become discouraged. And as I've suggested, many entertain significant doubts about the value of their recent participation in the public sphere. Whether they find new avenues of engagement or withdraw permanently to private life depends in part on the creativity and vision of the nation's peace, environmental, and social justice groups. It depends as well on whether these new participants can adopt the long view and develop the patience essential to continue even when their actions bear few or no immediate fruits. And it depends on whether they learn to savor both the journey of engagement itself and the everyday grace that nurtures us during the most difficult tasks. In "The Small Work in the Great Work," the Reverend Victoria Safford advises us to "plant ourselves at the gates of hope," even in times or situations that would invite pessimism, because "with our lives we make our answers all the time, to this ravenous, beautiful, mutilated, gorgeous world. . . ."

I like to think that something akin to this realization of the preciousness of life is what motivated Desmond Tutu when he joined the other dancers at the Los Angeles fundraising event. As the Polish poet Czeslaw Milosz has written, "There are nothing but gifts on this poor, poor earth." Tutu, like other social and political activists who haven't forgotten the importance of enjoyment, passionately embraces the gifts placed before him. If it's a gift of music, he will dance. If a gift of food, he will eat. If the company of friends, he will converse, laugh, and share stories. Such are the small but necessary pleasures that enable him to look evil in the eye and be confident that the fight must be fought. For only someone who knows how good life can be is in a position to appreciate what's at stake when life is degraded or destroyed.

Even if the struggle outlives us, even if it's impossible to envision a time when it will end, conviction matters. Actions of conscience confirm the link between our fate and that of everyone and everything else on the planet, respecting and reinforcing the fundamental connections without which life itself is impossible. Whether we flourish or perish depends on how well we understand and act in accordance with this interdependence—the same interdependence that Martin Luther King evoked: "We are caught in an inescapable network of mutuality tied in a single garment of destiny." In "From Hope to Hopelessness," Margaret Wheatley, author of *Turning to Each Other*, strips this notion to its essentials when she argues that only by renouncing the certainty that our actions will be effective can we continue on through hard times. So long as we are connected to our fellow human beings, Wheatley says, we can draw strength precisely from feeling "groundless, hopeless, insecure, patient, clear. And together. . . ."

HUMILITY AND DIGNITY

Perhaps humility is the most important lesson that this world's interdependence teaches us. Among other things, it counsels restraint. It says that giving up on life and the living is a form of arrogance. In "Only Justice Can Stop a Curse," Alice Walker examines the politics of bitterness, the temptation to conclude that we're destined for extinction: "Let the earth marinate in poisons. Let the bombs cover the ground like rain. For nothing short of total destruction will ever teach [us] anything." But then Walker remembers the acts of others that have given her cause to hope—and resolves that she will not be defeated by despair. What is this but a form of forgiveness? And everyone needs forgiveness—ourselves for not taking on every cause and winning every battle; and others, our neighbors and co-workers, our relatives and friends, and especially those who disagree with our beliefs or accept the lies and misdirections now so commonplace in our culture.

Nor should we forget that courage is contagious, that it overcomes the silence and fear that estrange people from one another. In Poland, during the early 1980s, leaders of the workers' support movement (KOR) made a point of printing their names and phone numbers on the back of mimeographed sheets describing incidents of police harassment against then unknown activists such as Lech Walesa. It was as if, in the words of reporter Lawrence Weschler, they were "calling out to everyone else, 'Come on out. Be open. What can they do to us if we all start taking responsibility for our true dreams?'"

As the Polish activists discovered, we gain something profound when we stand up for our beliefs, just as part of us dies when we know that something is wrong, yet do nothing. We could call this radical dignity. We don't have to tackle every issue, but if we avoid them all, if we remain silent in the face of cruelty, injustice, and oppression, we sacrifice part of our soul. In this sense, we keep on acting based on our conscience because by doing so we affirm our humanity, not only the core of who we are, but also what we hold in common with others.

_____ADDITIONAL READINGS_____

Brecher, Jeremy, Tim Costello, and Brendan Smith. 2002. *Globalization from Below: The Power of Solidarity.* Cambridge, MA: South End Press.

This book reveals and encourages the need for an emerging global movement to counteract the corporate-led global economic agenda.

Loeb, Paul Rogat. *Soul of a Citizen.* 1999. New York: St. Martin's.

Loeb's most comprehensive suggestions about the grit and character needed to participate as an active citizen in these difficult times.

Mertes, Tom (ed.). 2004. *A Movement of Movements.* New York: Verso Books.

Biographies and rationales of various anti-globalization activists and movements are put straight across here.

Tilly, Charles. 2004. *Social Movements, 1768–2004.* Boulder, CO: Paradigm Publishers.

A leading sociologist on the topic gives a sweeping history of social movements emphasizing their contributions to democracy and their changing forms in today's global system.